Drifted Sage Publishing

Design by Dakota Earth Cloud Walker

Sacred Heart Warrior

Language: English

ISBN-9781073549115

About Dakota Earth Cloud

I could list here all the training's I have taken over the past 30 years. I could tell you of all Shaman's I've worked with, I could share with you the years I spend as a Massage Therapist and then a Holistic Health Practitioner. I could tell you about the vision quests, the adventures I've taken in search of my soul. I could even tell you about the years I spent teaching and writing curriculum, and that my super powers lie in being able to get people from point A to point B. i could type out my resume, and for some that would seem impressive, interesting, and it would add credibility to my skill set.

But I'm not going to do that. If you want to know about my professional life, you can read it here.

So Who is Dakota Earth Cloud Walker? If not all those titles, labels, and accolades, then ... who are you?

Who am I?

Simply put, I am Dakota. I have dedicated my life to becoming the best version of myself, to live my soul's purpose – to find the exquisiteness of every moment. And in so many ways I succeed, and then, like you, I also experience the pains and falls that we all so often go through.

I am a passionate person, I put my entire heart into my work, and into my life. Someone recently said that it seems I have lived 22,000 lives in just this one lifetime. I think she is correct, or it feels right to me. I have had some of the most delicious experiences in my life – adventures, love, broken heart, heart cracked open, deep sorrow, encompassing joy and so much more. I take all this, and I pour it into my work, into my life and every day I look for the beauty, the lessons and the profound messages.

I am a teacher and a facilitator of soul change and growth. I have been most all of my life. I was born for this work. I am also a student, and everyday I take something new to marinate upon and soak up it's juicy lesson so that I can continue to grow myself.

I am grateful. I am grateful to be here, now, doing this and for being an active agent in this thing called life.

This Journal Belongs To:

....

Date:

....

Acknowledgements

I acknowledge you. The seeker in you, the dreamer, the wise one, the curious one, the one who loves deeply and passionately. The part of you that is rising up and becoming the best version of you. I acknowledge the pain and sorrow, the suffering that it took for you to get where you are today. I acknowledge the extreme amount of strength it took for you to pull yourself out of those darkest moments and make your way here, to this moment, to this path. You are a unique expression of God, of Spirit, of the Universe and inside you is a vast amount of energy—untapped, raw, and ready to be birthed. I see you, I am witnessing you, I acknowledge the imprint you are leaving in my world and am grateful to share this moment with you.

Aho Mitakuye Oyasin

	Content	Page

Gaia Wisdom Shamanic Mentorship

An online training program that teaches you to live more fully, authentically, and with the deep wisdom held within you. A program to assist you in walking your shamanic path through the powerful tool of the Medicine Wheel.

Learn More or Enroll in the Program Online at:
www.dakotaearthcloud.com

What is the Shaman's Path?

Most often, we associate Shamans with elders within indigenous cultures who might wear masks and dance to the tribe's drumbeat while they journey to other worlds to help heal those in the tribe who are sick. In historical context, this is true. Shamans were the healers and seers for the tribe.

In the modern day where we live today, **we have become severely cut off from the old ways** and more disconcerting, cut off from our own deep wisdom. Technology has replaced our connection to nature, ego and materialism punctuates a state of fear and want that is hard to dismantle, addictions keep us numbed out, and for most, there is not a tribal shaman with whom we can seek healing.

For those of us who have kept the old ways alive in our soul, we have found our way back to the shamanic path. A path where we are deeply connected within our soul to the divine source. **We walk deliberately,** and with attention and intention. We strive to be **authentic, truthful, curious, and our own healer.** We step into our power and manifest our lives in a beautiful and abundant way that is reflective of our core.

> *"The Medicine Wheel is a powerful container for organizing our lives, for gaining greater perspective, and for working with the energy of the directions to find harmony and balance. It is by far, the most powerful tool in navigating the Shaman's Path."*
>
> *Dakota*

Walking the Shamanic Path takes courage, patience, mindfulness, openness, and a willingness to no longer play small but to stand up and claim your spot as a warrior for the old ways, to be a change maker and an advocate for expansion and love.

Using the Medicine Wheel for Healing

Like Shamanism, the Medicine Wheel spans our historical records for thousands of years. Stone circles, similar to the Native American Medicine Wheel, were long used for healing, ritual, and ceremony.

The Medicine Wheel is the foundation of the Gaia Wisdom Shamanic Mentorship. **It provides a powerful container to gain better perspective and understanding of various situations in our lives.** When you begin walking the Wheel, you carry with you the energy and power from the Directions of the Medicine Wheel. Learning how to use these energies as allies, you gain more control over your own path.

The Medicine Wheel is divided into 7 directions. The 4 cardinal directions are North, South, East, and West. You also have the Center/Space Within an Father Sky and Mother Earth. **Once we have learned how to use the Medicine Wheel as a tool, we are able to stand in the Center/ Space Within and pull the energy as needed from the various directions. We can intuitively know what we need to gain more of, or let go in order to find harmony and balance.**

Learn and Explore at Your Pace

The Gaia Wisdom Shamanic Mentorship is separated into **4 sessions, one for each direction/season. We open enrollment 4 times a year January, March, June, and September.** The course is entirely online and as long as you have an internet connection, you can take the course.

Learn About Each Session Below

> *"People don't need to be saved, or rescued. They just need access to soul tools, (perhaps long forgotten), that allow them to rediscover exactly how powerful, brilliant, and authentic they are. To learn how to heal past wounds or blocks that keep them tethered to an unhappy life. To be challenged in a way that is both honoring, enlightening and transformative. This is my Sacred Purpose, this is my soul calling – to assist others to step up and find their soul's purpose so they can help influence the world in their own beautiful way."*
>
> **Dakota Earth Cloud Walker**

- Each session runs for **9 weeks** (see the sessions below for details on individual sessions)
- Each session includes **9 guided, shamanic meditations** that coincide with the specific session you are enrolled in.
- You will also have **3 Bonus Meditations** to begin immediately upon enrolling.
- Each week you will have **teaching and soul work units** opened for you to explore. Some weeks you may have one of each while other weeks there are 2-3 units.
- Each lesson has a **written packet on a particular topic, and soul work** to allow you to go deeper and to integrate into your life.
- We have a **weekly 1.5-hour work-shopping and integration call.** We'll discuss the week's work, answer questions, and have exercises to strengthen what you are learning. (All calls are recorded if you miss it). Calls are on **Thursday's.**
- You will be enrolled in the **Introduction to the Medicine Wheel** course and will have immediate access to this course upon enrollment.
- You receive a comprehensive **Energy Assessment Tool** which tracks your soul growth from one direction to the next.
- You will also have **access to the vault of resources,** additional recommendations.
- Wisdom Keeper (year long) enrollees will receive **4 additional courses; Dreaming Our Soul Home, Sacred Purpose: The Divine Plan; Awakening the Sacred Heart; and Nuts & Bolts to Shamanic Journeying.**
- Wisdom Keepers are also enrolled in our **Gaia Meditation Club,** receiving a weekly guided meditation.
- Wisdom Keepers have a **live workshop once monthly** where participants learn how to bring all the energies of each direction together to live a more integrated life and to take the teachings to apply them to real-world scenarios.

As a Mentorship student, you will receive a **significant discount on all meditation purchases.**

Is this Shamanic Training for Me?

The short answer, yes.

How do I know if I need this program?

There are "markers" in our lives to show us when we are living our soul's purpose, or not. If you can answer the following statements with a resounding Yes! then this program would help you stay on that course. If you cannot answer yes to most, then this program will help you find your shamanic voice and path.

- I am deeply connected to my spiritual path and know definitively what I believe and why.
- I have a strong relationship with my spirit guides, higher self, and source.
- I love myself completely and fully and actively do things to take care of myself.
- My relationships to others are sacred, conscious, and connected.
- I am surrounded by love, joy, and I feel balanced in all areas of my life.
- I have found my sacred purpose in work and love the job I have.
- I speak with confidence, with compassion, and with thoughtfulness.
- I have a healthy self-esteem but am aware of my ego.
- I tell myself loving thoughts and kind words, I dwell in the present moment.
- I communicate clearly, and consciously.
- I am creative, vibrant, and intuitive.
- I spend quality time in nature, connecting to the elements and to nature.
- I feel nurtured by the space I live in, it reflects my personality and spirituality.
- I allow my emotions to be felt fully, not repressing them or allowing them to overcome me.
- I eat healthy, nutritious meals and take care of my physical well being.
- I am the healthiest person I know.
- I have forgiven those in my life who have wronged me, including myself.
- I practice daily gratitude and acts of kindness.
- I have a daily spiritual practice that sustains me.

That is a healthy list of items that we all aspire to master in our one life here. In the Gaia Wisdom Shamanic Mentorship, we methodically go through each direction and balance the energy and in doing so, we hit every single thing on the list above.

How to get the most from this journal ....

Write in it! Draw, scribble, wander, let it all spill out! As we go through the 9 weeks of the Mentorship, let this be your companion. Use markers or colored pencils and color in the images. If you are a Mentorship Student, take notes on the course work and during the live calls. Fill in the calendar with important reminders, like the live calls and when you'll do some self care. Record your experiences of the meditations. Create goals for the 9 weeks but also for one week at a time. Get inspired, share how you use this journal with your community.

For the Next 12 Weeks of the South Direction
(some gentle reminders)

- Be gentle with yourself
- Get plenty of good sleep
- Drink a lot of water, eat healthy foods
- Take yourself on Soul Dates
- Lean into the community
- Show up as much as you can
- Allow yourself to take risks
- Move, exercise, get outside and enjoy nature
- Meditate
- Be curious
- Keep a beginners mind
- Do the work ... even when it pains you

How are you committed to caring for yourself?

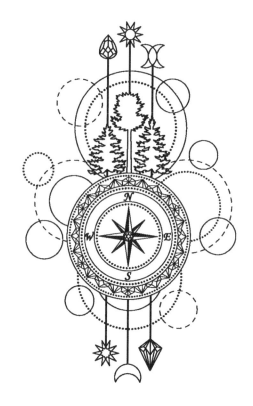

Prayer for the Directions

By Dakota Earth Cloud Walker

I call upon the spirit of the East,

A place of new beginnings, a new life, and a new birth.

I clear my mind so that I may be inspired.

I open this space for new ideas to be born, that I may have the knowledge and clarity for them to sprout. Eagle;

please carry my ideas and dreams safely on your wings.

And to Owl, may you plant within me the seeds needed for new dreams.

I am grateful.

I call upon the spirit of the South,

a place of expression and creativity, passion and play.

Allow me to feel your fullness, your richness, and your warmth.

In this space I nurture my dreams and watch as your energy helps them to grow and expand.

Please open my intuition so that I may express with my soul.

I call upon Dolphin, to safely swim in the warm waters that carry my dreams

And for Frog to teach me the patience I may need.

I am grateful.

I call upon the spirit of the West,

In this space where my dreams transform into conscious reality

I call upon your energy now

Please come into this sacred space and allow me to discover myself and each other

I call upon the Phoenix to transform me through his sacred fires

And to the snake, may she be the keeper of my dreamtime as I shed my skin.

I am grateful

To my ancestors of the North

I call upon your wise council and ask for your guidance.

Bring me to my death and to my rebirth.

Allow me to bear witness to the cycle of completion.

May I travel inward to hear your loving guidance.

I call upon Bear to watch over me and infuse me with his power

And to Turtle, I ask you for the blessings from heaven and earth.

I am grateful

Grandfather Sky

You are the breath of my life and I send my prayers to your safe heavens.

I ask for your loving energy to connect me to my soul family where I may

Experience the Oneness of this great Universe.

I am grateful

Grandmother Earth

Your loving home surrounds and supports me.

I call upon Gaia to awaken within me the eternal understanding, respect and unconditional love.

Mother Earth may you feel my feet deeply rooted as I tread gently upon your flesh.

May we nurture and honor one another for as long as I remain in this earthly body, and beyond.

I am grateful.

To the Spirit Within Me

I call upon my emerging soul, the essence of all that is.

May the butterfly land gently on my spirit and carry with it the song of my soul

to all those here and beyond.

I am all that I am and I am grateful.

Embracing the Sacred Heart Warrior

In the hour of the noon-time sun, on the day of the Summer Solstice, and during the prime of our young adulthood, the South Direction or also known as Alban Hefin, Light of the Shore, in Celtic traditions, is in its full force.

When a person reaches into their memory bank of earlier summers, often what is reflected are the times of summer vacations, playing in the waves of the ocean or swimming in a lake and finding yourself soaking up the warm rays of the sun. Fun, laughter, playfulness, and even sexual energy are often embedded into these long-ago summer experiences. Within each of us is some fond recollection of these moments and brings us back to a feeling of "the good ole days." When I asked a group of students to reflect on their feelings of summer, these memories were the most prominent and yet followed by a reflection of sadness that "those days" were long gone. Summers carried a different vibration for them now than it did when they were in their late childhood or young adulthood. Innocence was replaced by responsibility, the laughter replaced by stress and worry, the playfulness replaced by the mandates of a "real adult life." How often do we deny ourselves permission to be mischievous, playful, and spontaneous? We find ourselves feeling the burden of not wanting to appear childish or immature, so we adopt a more grown up persona that edges out the creativity, and brilliance that the South Direction exudes.

The energy of the South Direction invokes the emotional and intuitive bodies. It begs us to feel, rather than to think and asks us to express ourselves through more creative outlets – dancing, singing, play, art, lovemaking, nature and more. If we likened it to the dynamics of a family where everyone has a "role", the South would be the joker, the light-hearted one, the life of the family.

The Goddess of the South

She will take you to the lake and entice you to skinny dip, telling you that the reason she strips her clothes off is so she can feel the cool, fresh water next to her skin. She will lie on a warm rock in the hot sun and marry herself to Mother Earth and Father Sky. She will let the warmth of the sun penetrate through her bones and into the marrow of her beingness. Next she will bring out a vibrant, colorful tapestry sewn together by her own hands and gently lay a feast of gorgeous foods from her garden.... bright red tomatoes, deep green cucumbers, a bowl of the sweetest blackberries and raspberries. She will pluck a berry into her mouth and take several minutes to consume just one. She wants the richness out of every succulent bite and doesn't want to miss a single moment of its sweetness. Her laugh comes from the center of joy, and she tells stories of love and sorrow. She feels the spectrum of emotion, sometimes simultaneously and other times over the course of stringed together moments. When grief comes, you will witness her plunge into it and as she moves through it, you watch the wave bring her back up to her center point. At the end of the afternoon she swoops you up in her arms and begins dancing and singing, moving the two of you together in perfect rhythm with the earth. The Nature Spirits begin to come out from their hiding places, dancing and frolicking among the trees and flowers, often mimicking the two of you. Somewhere in the hours you spend with this lovely divine being, you begin feeling a tiny prick of emotion waking up inside of you. As it begins to blossom and unfold, a sense of knowing envelops you. You have been here before, it says. And you know the voice is correct. You have been here, you once danced and sang, swam naked in the waters, and tasted life fully. As this remembrance strengthens, you call out to the spirits of the South. "Come open me up," you plea. The dolphin jumps out of the water and brings you the lightness of play and primes your sense of awareness. The frog hops out from under the large leaves of a nearby plant and brings patience. The Salmon leaps through the rapids of a nearby river, imparting the keys to deep wisdom. From a distance, you hear the howling of a coyote, and you are reminded once again to play and to learn how to adapt to different situations. Finally, a woodpecker flies to a nearby tree. "Cuk Cuk Cuk Cuk" he rattles off as he pecks at the trunk of the old giant. In his song, he reminds you of the importance of being close to Mother Nature, to drum more and sync your heartbeat to hers.

In this colorful menagerie of helping spirits, you get a sense that you are never alone, nor are you ever far from the energy the South Direction brings. You have longed for this energy, to crack your heart open and step confidently into its unknown depths. This is where the juiciness of life is, she tells you. Your dreams and visions are grown in the fields of your open heart, watered by the emotions of curiosity, power, determination, love, and trust and fertilized by that small still voice inside of you that speaks the wisdom of the salmon and your guides.
A small part of you resists though. And she senses this.

You state your objections to living life fully. "I have doubts; I feel disconnected; I feel guilty." She sees beyond the veil of what is and can see you have disconnected from your Higher Self, and that you are hiding behind drama and emotions. She sees all how you keep yourself distracted from the deeper emotions in your heart. She tells you that forgiveness is a gift you give to yourself, to free yourself from the bounds of energy which no longer serve you. Again, you know she is right. You know all of these things because there is a part of you that has kept the door ajar just enough.

With emotions overflowing, you drop to your knees and feel your brow pressed up against the cool rich, fertile soil of Mother Earth. You begin shedding tears that seem as ancient as your soul, uncontrollable tears streaming down your face and into the soil. It starts as a small push against your forehead, and then you feel an essence begin to emerge from the earth where your tears fall. Before you can even speak a word, you find yourself witnessing the Goddess Danu standing before you. Danu, the most ancient of all Celtic Deities, is considered the Great Mother of Ireland, an Earth Goddess, a Triple Goddess of the Maiden, the Crone, and the Divine Lady. You feel her immense power in the air, streaming through the earth, and flowing through the waters.

She places her hands on your heart and tells you she is here to impart her knowledge, wisdom, and to be a teacher. She will help you to find abundance, in all aspects. She tells you that you are a part of the Tuatha de Dannan, which means the "Children of Danu." These are the wise ones, she tells you.

She asks you, "How can I be of service?" and you begin to tell her all the things in your heart. You tell her of all the ways you fail to love yourself or to love others unconditionally. You tell her about the fear that blocks you from moving into your sacred purpose, and the fear that keeps your heart closed off to others. Fear of rejection, fear of loneliness, fear of love. You tell her your feelings of being powerless, and small, sometimes even insignificant. She continues to listen deeply. You speak of the times you have felt numb, and far removed from the richness of an embodied life. You share with her your struggles to live a creative and juicy life when debts and obligations are lingering in the fringes of your life. And when you feel you have shared all your struggles, worries, fears, blocks and more, she sits with you in silence, offering nothing more than quiet space for your spirit of acknowledging all this and more. You feel the lightness of her touch and the profoundness of her presence as she offers to clear you of your stagnant energy and to remove any blockages so that your efforts will easily flow into fruition. With this promise,

you feel a renewed sense of hope and motivation.

She reminds you of the power to create the life you desire already resides within you. For a moment, she gives you a glimpse of your Ascended Self, and you feel that she is indeed correct, you are reminded of the wisdom you have inside. In her presence, you feel worthy and capable of realizing your dreams. She assures you that you will not be alone on your quest to realign with your Divine Truth.

She invites you to listen closely to spirits, the earth, and nature all around you. "Do you hear it?" She asks. You listen closer, not quite sure what you are hearing, but it has the faint sounds of a beautiful melody.

She touches your heart once more, and you feel a wider opening, suddenly the sound becomes more distinct and louder. It's music, beautiful melodious music.

"What is that song?" you ask. "It is the song inside you," she answers. She and the maiden of the South Direction begin singing, and soon all the forest spirits are singing as well. The music makes you happy, and you feel that well of joy inside.

"You must learn to sing this song," and with that, she and the maiden of the South Direction and all the forest spirits slowly disappear into the light. Noon turns to dusk, summer shifts into Autumn, and we move into our older adulthood, taking with us the powers and energies of the South Direction.

An Imbalance in Energy

The story above illustrates many of the energies you can expect to encounter as you walk through the South Direction. These energies can work together or can utilize individual energies, but the power and strength come truly, from being able to integrate multiple energies simultaneously. Let's work with a real-life scenario to illustrate this point.

Sue, a longtime client, has had struggles within her marriage to Jerry. She is a confessed workaholic and often works upward of 60 hours a week. It has taken a toll on the marriage but also in all her relationships. When asked about her emotional state, Sue states that she "holds it all in" because to allow the overwhelming stress surface that she feels daily would send her, and Jerry, both over the edge. When I ask about taking time out to play or go on dates or what she does that might be considered spontaneous, "Yeah, right!" as she laughs and shrugs off the ideas. Sue is exhibiting classic excess energy in the East Direction with a deficiency of energy in the South. If the energy is deficient in one area, it must shift to a different direction where it becomes excess energy. When we begin to unravel the story further, we learn that Sue not only tampers down her emotions, but she is disconnected from her intuition as well. As a result, there becomes a deficiency of energy in the North Direction as well. Using the example of a balloon being pushed in on one side pushes the air in excess to another area. With two directions deficient you will now see two directions in excess. When you begin to look at the energy of the West Direction, Sue has chronic headaches; she often uses wine to "relax," her doctor has her on blood pressure medicine, and she indicates that she is often on the verge of blowing up. She feels stuck in the cycle because she is the primary caregiver of the family and is responsible for the financial aspect of their life together. This, to many degrees, causes resentment and the never-ending struggle she feels of not being able to do what she truly loves.

Looking at the Directions once more, let's do a refresher. The East is the mental body and our career house for Sacred Purpose. This is where Sue has an excess, and we know this because she resides in the mental body and is a workaholic. The West is our physical body and environmental house. Her excess energy shows up in the form of health problems, addictions (wine), her inability to see a way out (transformation, death, and rebirth), and the financial burden.

To help Sue find the balance, we need to shift the excess energy from the East and West to the North and South. I am a big believer in making small changes often rather than making huge changes all at once.

There are many changes which can be made, that would help Sue to balance her energy and truly you would work multiple energies from all the directions to enable this. From an esoteric point of view, if we were to just tap into the South Direction's energy we may call in the energy of the dolphin, and ask for our awareness to be heightened so we can begin seeing how the energy is being played out. Calling on Frog because, in times where a lot of change needs to happen, patience is a must. Leaning into the energy of the Goddess Danu to reconnect us to earth, and nature will help us to open more clearly to our intuition which in turns helps balance the North as we reconnect to our Spirit Guides. With access to our Spirit Guides again and our intuition, we can then start harnessing that energy to forge a path for ourselves. Next, we might call on the Coyote to help us to lighten up, have some humor and some fun in life which helps take some of the stress away from the East – minimizes the impact of being a workaholic. And eventually, by adding more play into life, we become healthier – blood pressure lowers, Sue needs less wine to relax, and by feeling better physically, we tend to take care of ourselves more. When we care for our physical body, we become lighter, and that lightness often translates into a healthier emotional body as well.

From a practical, more logical point of view, we can harness the power of the south energy by raising our emotional intelligence and healing trapped emotions that we've held onto for years. We utilize the creative outlets for various emotions and recover our sense of self through acts of self-love and trusting our intuition. We can deepen our relationships through solid tools built for creating a heart-centered connection to another human.

Do you see where I am going with all this? It's a dance, sometimes a very deliberate dance where you must learn all the steps and perform them in order while other times you are freestyling the moves and following one move into the next.

To know which dance needs to perform, you have first to know what shape your balloon is. Ideally, you would assess each of the directions because that will paint a broader picture for yourself and one that helps you to determine if you need to dance the Salsa or if throwing your arms up in the air and moving to the beat is more your style. For now, we are going to assess your South Direction to determine if you are in excess or deficient.

Draw or describe your altar ... what would you add and why? What does each item mean to you? If you cannot make a physical alter, use this space to paste photos of what you would include.

Your Sacred Heart Warrior Altar

With each direction, we have new energy to work with and to connect fully to that energy, create an altar that reflects the Sacred Heart Warrior/South Direction. Whether you are experiencing winter (those south of the equator) or summer (north of the equator) we will still be working with this South energy these next 9 weeks.

Choose a place where you can spend time alone with your altar, you may want to meditate near it, or do your course work nearby, or even write in this journal. Create this first sacred space so that you have a "go to" place to retreat, refuel, and reconnect.

Your altar is personal to you. Although I will give you some ideas of things you may want to place on your altar for this specific direction, use your discretion and if something feels like it needs to be there then add it. If something from this list doesn't feel right, then don't add it. This is one way we empower ourselves, by creating the space that is as unique as our fingerprint. No one can tell you what you should or shouldn't do—this is your journey, your path, your altar.

Once you have completed your altar, if you feel inclined, share a photo of it with the community. We can always inspire one another by seeing how others create their sacred space.

Elements of the Sacred Heart Warrior

(These are ideas, symbols, items you may want to include in your sacred space to draw in the energy of the South.) The meaning of Water moves the emotional body, adds flow to your life. It's the element of depth, cleansing, nurturing, and has deep, symbolic meaning.

- Tobacco (sacred herb of the South)
- Water (element, may use holy water, a chalice, stones from a river, sand or shells from ocean.)
- Spirit Guides/Spiritual Realm (might include totems of power animals, items reminding you of your guides, etc.)
- Summer (items depicting summer— creativity, passion, movement, water, growth, nurturing.)
- Lantern or candle (often used as a "guiding light" for your guides to feel welcomed).
- Frog, Dolphin and Salmon are the guardian animals of the South so anything which represents these animals.
- Young adulthood (something reminding you of your connection to your young adulthood and that part of you full of dreams and inspiration.)
- Something representing your emotional and intuitive bodies—a photo, something sentimental given to you.

How to Get the Most From this Guided Journal

The Sacred Heart Warrior Journal

Carefully plotted out to follow the course of the South Direction of the Medicine Wheel and to guide you to the inner-most parts of your heart, this journal will assist you in gaining more awareness of the energy the Sacred Heart Warrior brings. By the time you finish these 3 months, you will have a soul-filled journal and a heightened awareness of self-love, emotional congruency, your relationships, intuition, and much, much more.

Things I will do this month to create more joy and love in the world.

HEALTH & WELLNESS	FAMILY & FRIENDS
SELF-LOVE	ROMANCE & RELATIONSHIPS
SPIRITUAL PRACTICES	JOB & CAREER

Intentions and Goals

Each Month, create one focus/goal that you would like to specifically work towards. This sets your intention for the month. You'll also be able to create goals in each of the areas of your life. Getting clear about what you would like to achieve is the first step towards realizing your goals and dreams. The East Direction of the Medicine Wheel is the energy we use in creating these goals, the South Direction is the energy needed to nurture them and bring them to life.

The "Get To" Lists

In your weekly overview, you have space for your "Get To Do" list. Our words have power and by shifting our vocabulary from "have to do" to "get to do" will shift your mood from negative to positive. Each week, make your lists of all the things you get to do that will help nurture your life and bring balance, movement, abundance and more to your life.

Tracking Emotions

In the South Direction, there is much emphasis on our emotional body and building our emotional intelligence muscle. At the end of each day, return to your weekly overview page and write in the dominant emotion you felt that day. This helps you to become more aware of the emotions arising throughout your day but also gives you a starting place to notice patterns and repeat offenders. If, for example, every Monday your dominant emotion is overwhelmed, it gives you a clue to look at what happens on Monday that might not happen the other days. From there, you can make tiny shifts.

EMOTION CHECK IN

What emotion ruled your day?

 overwhelm

 content

 frustration

The Check-In

WHAT AM I NURTURING THIS WEEK?

Focusing on my diet and body this week. Healthy foods, meditation, and exercise.

WEEKLY SOUL TRACKER

	M	T	W	T	F	S	S
LOVED MYSELF	✓	✓			✓		✓
BUILT CONNECTION		✓		✓			
FED MY SOUL		✓		✓		✓	
ATE HEALTHY	✓	✓	✓	✓		✓	

MY REWARD: Get a massage

Each week, choose a seed you would like to nurture. These can be related to your monthly goals/intentions and turned into micro goals or action steps to keep you moving towards your overall dream.

In the South Direction, the dominant energy is "nurturing" and you can also track how well you do in nurturing your self-love muscle, relationships, and bringing vibrancy into your life. If you wish, choose a reward for yourself if you meet your nurturing goals by at least 80%. It's important to reward ourselves, and have fun (another attribute of the South)

The Challenge and Questions

DAILY LOVE WARRIOR CHALLENGE:

Create an altar for the South Direction. Use things that symbolize the various energies of the South. Put in a space wher

Each week follows a different "theme" and each day you will receive both a challenge and a reflective question for that day and that theme. Use the questions as a reflection at the end of your day.

DAILY LOVE REFLECTIVE QUESTI

When do

Weekly Review: At the end of your week, do a check in with yourself to see how you grew and flourished, and where you might have been challenged.

What I Learned

Meditating in the morning made the rest of the day feel more connected. I found a lot of inspiration once I began seeking it out. I need to get better at journaling my journey.

My Big Win's

I meditated 5 full days. I had a 5 hour Soul Date. Date Night was a success! I didn't have any wine 4 nights.

My Challenges

I found it hard to breathe deeply—will work on it. Also fell asleep most nights before I could read or set intentions. Couldn't remember dreams. Will try going to bed earlier next week.

Sum Up This Week in 4-5 Words

 Inspiring

Rituals & Medicine Wheel Energy

Using the energies of the Medicine Wheel, make plans to meet the needs of the Wheel within your life.

Use the Medicine Wheel to plan out rituals, activities, energies you want to tap into as you navigate this week.

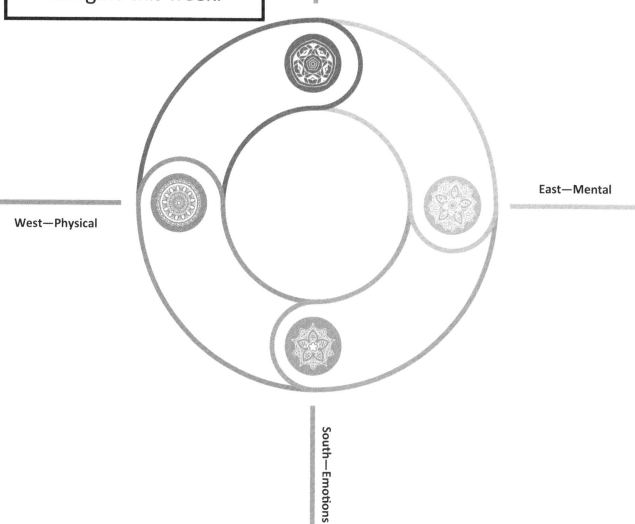

North—Spiritual

East—Mental

West—Physical

South—Emotions

Rituals & Medicine Wheel Energy

Using the energies of the Medicine Wheel, make plans to meet the needs of the Wheel within your life.

North—Spiritual

Night Rituals:

6 deep abdominal breaths before bed.

Read a poem from Embers book or David Whyte.

Write intention for dreamtime.

Morning Rituals:

Meditation

Review Schedule for week/Day

Morning Mantras

Review Goals and plan tiny steps or action steps I can take today.

East—Mental

Look for signs daily record here..

West—Physical

This week I'm balancing the energy at work

Sample Page

Evening Rituals:

Gratitude at dinner with partner.

Journal my reflections from today—assess and document energy flow.

Afternoon Rituals:

Look for inspiration throughout day and take photos

Gratitude: Make it a point this week to tell one person why I am grateful for them.

South—Emotions

Color—paying attention to colors this week and how they make me feel.

Soul Date Plan:

....

....

....

....

....

Self Love:

....

....

....

....

....

Self Care:

....

....

....

....

....

Relationship to Self

Connect With:

....

....

....

....

....

Nurture:

....

....

....

....

....

Set Boundaries:

....

....

....

....

....

Relationship to Others

Start:

....

....

....

....

....

Continue On:

....

....

....

....

....

Finish:

....

....

....

....

....

Relationship to Goals

WEEKLY OVERVIEW

WORK
GET TO DO LIST
- ✓ Send emails about class
- ✓ Finish billing
- ✓ Make web changes
- ○ Map out proposal
- ○ Meet with staff
- ○

PERSONAL
GET TO DO LIST
- ✓ Get hair cut
- ○ Schedule massage
- ✓ Write Mom
- ✓ Get b-day gift/Kym
- ○ Wash dogs
- ✓ Call insurance company

SELF-LOVE
GET TO DO LIST
- ✓ Soul Date Monday
- ✓ Pick 3 new recipes
- ○ Say no to extra work
- ✓ Meditate 15 minutes a day
- ○
- ○

Order the cookbook Danielle suggested.

Coffee with Lori on Tuesday?

Offer Wags and Wine Wednesday to the staff at complex.

EMOTION CHECK IN

What emotion ruled your day?

- M — overwhelm
- T — content
- W — frustration
- T — gratitude
- F — happy
- S — focused
- S — peace

WHAT AM I NURTURING THIS WEEK?

Focusing on my diet and body this week. Healthy foods, meditation, and exercise.

WEEKLY SOUL TRACKER

	M	T	W	T	F	S	S
LOVED MYSELF	✓	✓		✓		✓	
BUILT CONNECTION		✓	✓	✓			
FED MY SOUL	✓		✓		✓		
ATE HEALTHY	✓	✓	✓	✓	✓		

MY REWARD: Get a massage

Big Gratitude: For joining the Mentorship and the community

Empowering

I felt empowered today when I faced my fear and asked for a raise. I feel like I deserve it given how much I give to this job. Mike considered it thoughtfully and agreed that I do deserve more and is willing to see what is in the company budget. It felt great to be my own champion and to stand up for what I feel I am worth. I gave myself a voice today.

I'd like to empower myself more by creating a business plan to open my own business someday.

I loved well by ... Not having as much chocolate as I wanted to have :)

I nurtured my body by eating a healthier meal and taking the time to acknowledge the food as a blessing. I nurtured my soul this morning when I took a soul date and tended to my own joys and needs. I nurtured my relationships by being present with my friends at girls night out. I nurtured my mind during the conference, asking questions instead of being to afraid to speak up. I am going to nurture the dream of the Scotland trip after getting intuitive messages today regarding that **dream.**

Nurturing

Date:

MORNING MANTRA/PRAYER:

I am finding love in unexpected places

TODAY

05
06
07
08 Doctor's appt
09 Soul Date
10
11
12
01 Women of Inspiration
02 Conference
03
04
05
06
07 Girls night out
08
09
10
11
12

○ Mary
✓ Dakota
○
○
○
○
○

✓ Cable company
✓ Mom
○
○
○
○
○

SELF LOVE/CARE

Ate healthy today. Spent time meditating and journaling

INTUITIVE MESSAGES

Explore the Scotland trip, call the tax lady.

TODAY'S GRATITUDE: For the laughter Navi created in me.

DAILY LOVE WARRIOR CHALLENGE:

Face one of your fears today. It could be a small fear or a bigger one but make one step towards facing and conquering this fear that has held you back or holds you back from living life fully.

Faced my fear of rejection and asked for a raise at work.

DAILY LOVE REFLECTIVE QUESTION:

How have your fears held you back? What would you do if fear was not facing you?

They have kept me from going further than I am. I stop short of growing out of fear. If I step past that point of fear, I could do more at work and in my role as a manager.

Your Adventure Starts Now

I want to

- ◯ TO FEEL
- ◯ TO FINISH
- ◯ TO MAKE
- ◯ TO LEARN

So I can get

- ◯ MORE
- ◯ LESS
- ◯ BETTER
- ◯ ACCESS

Inspirations and Notes

Month/Year:

MONDAY	TUESDAY	WEDNESDAY	THURSDAY	FRIDAY	SATURDAY	SUNDAY

Top Goals

Things I will do this month to create more joy and love in the world.

....

....

....

....

....

....

....

....

....

....

....

HEALTH & WELLNESS

FAMILY & FRIENDS

SELF-LOVE

ROMANCE & RELATIONSHIPS

SPIRITUAL PRACTICES

JOB & CAREER

I want to

- ⬤ TO FEEL
- ⬤ TO FINISH
- ⬤ TO MAKE
- ⬤ TO LEARN

So I can get

- ⬤ MORE
- ⬤ LESS
- ⬤ BETTER
- ⬤ ACCESS

Inspirations and Notes

Month/Year:

MONDAY	TUESDAY	WEDNESDAY	THURSDAY	FRIDAY	SATURDAY	SUNDAY

Top Goals

Things I will do this month to create more joy and love in the world.

....

....

....

....

HEALTH & WELLNESS	FAMILY & FRIENDS

....

....

....

SELF-LOVE	ROMANCE & RELATIONSHIPS

....

....

....

SPIRITUAL PRACTICES	JOB & CAREER

I want to

- ⬤ TO FEEL
- ⬤ TO FINISH
- ⬤ TO MAKE
- ⬤ TO LEARN

So I can get

- ⬤ MORE
- ⬤ LESS
- ⬤ BETTER
- ⬤ ACCESS

Inspirations and Notes

Month/Year:

MONDAY	TUESDAY	WEDNESDAY	THURSDAY	FRIDAY	SATURDAY	SUNDAY

Top Goals

Things I will do this month to create more joy and love in the world.

....

....

....

....

....

....

....

....

....

....

....

....

HEALTH & WELLNESS

FAMILY & FRIENDS

SELF-LOVE

ROMANCE & RELATIONSHIPS

SPIRITUAL PRACTICES

JOB & CAREER

The Sacred Heart Warrior

For the next 12 weeks, you will be immersed in the energy of the South Direction of the Medicine Wheel. This is a vibrant time, full of creativity and aliveness. It's an emotional haven that will roll you around in the warm waters of joy, love, fear, and everything in between. Each week we will follow a different energy of the direction. In this first week, we prepare for the opening and the journey ...

Put yourself at the top of your to-do list every single day and the rest will fall into place.

Medicine Wheel Cheat Sheet

Listed below are the primary energies for each of the cardinal directions. Use these energies or find ways to bring the energy of a direction into your rituals and practices. Create rituals for day/week/month that you can use to keep the energy of all the directions in balance.

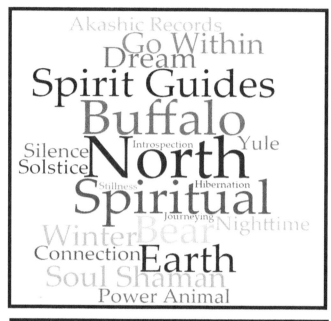

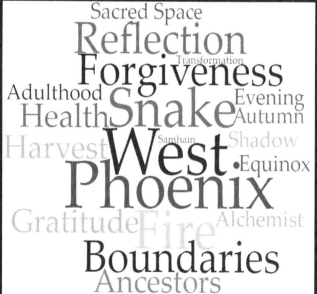

Rituals and Medicine Wheel Energy

Using the energies of the Medicine Wheel, make plans to meet the needs of the Wheel within your life.

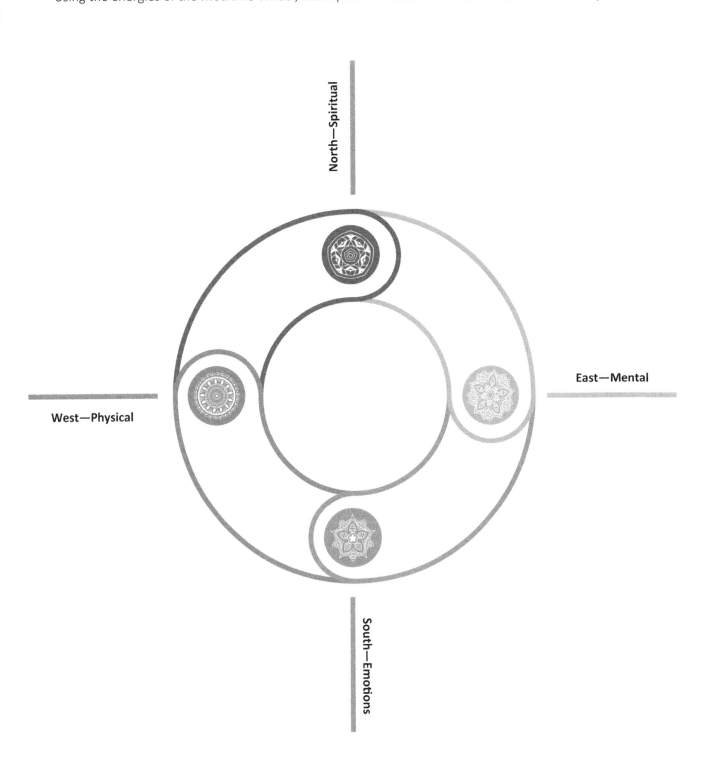

Soul Date Plan:

....

....

....

....

....

Self Love:

....

....

....

....

....

Self Care:

....

....

....

....

....

Relationship to Self

Connect With:

....

....

....

....

....

Nurture:

....

....

....

....

....

Set Boundaries:

....

....

....

....

....

Relationship to Others

Start:

....

....

....

....

....

Continue On:

....

....

....

....

....

Finish:

....

....

....

....

....

Relationship to Goals

WEEKLY OVERVIEW

WORK
GET TO DO LIST

PERSONAL
GET TO DO LIST

SELF-LOVE
GET TO DO LIST

EMOTION CHECK IN

What emotion ruled your day?

M
T
W
T
F
S
S

WHAT AM I NURTURING THIS WEEK?

WEEKLY SOUL TRACKER

	M	T	W	T	F	S	S
LOVED MYSELF							
BUILT CONNECTION							
FED MY SOUL							
ATE HEALTHY							

MY REWARD:

Big Gratitude:

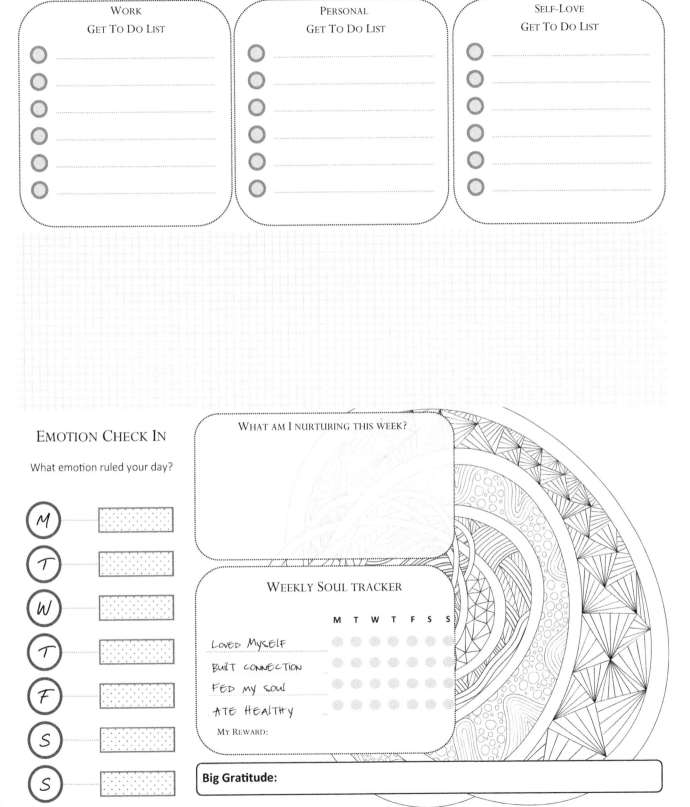

Empowering

I am ...

Nurturing

Date:

TODAY

MORNING MANTRA/PRAYER:

05 ....

06 ....

07 ....

08 ....

09 ....

10 ....

11 ....

12 ....

01 ....

02 ....

03 ....

04 ....

05 ....

06 ....

07 ....

08 ....

09 ....

10 ....

11 ....

12 ....

SELF LOVE/CARE

INTUITIVE MESSAGES

TODAY'S GRATITUDE:

DAILY LOVE WARRIOR CHALLENGE:

Create an altar for the South Direction. Use things that symbolize the various energies of the South. Put in a space where you can use it for sacred time for yourself.

DAILY LOVE REFLECTIVE QUESTION:

When do you feel most creative?

Empowering

I learned ...

Nurturing

Date:

TODAY

05
06
07
08
09
10
11
12
01
02
03
04
05
06
07
08
09
10
11
12

MORNING MANTRA/PRAYER:

SELF LOVE/CARE

INTUITIVE MESSAGES

TODAY'S GRATITUDE:

DAILY LOVE WARRIOR CHALLENGE:

Create a ceremony/ritual to open the South Direction for yourself. You can use the elements of the South, symbols, whatever feels right to you. This is your ceremony ...

DAILY LOVE REFLECTIVE QUESTION:

Give an honest assessment about your current relationships.

Empowering

I loved well by ...

Nurturing

Date:

TODAY

MORNING MANTRA/PRAYER:

05
06
07
08
09
10
11
12
01
02
03
04
05
06
07
08
09
10
11
12

SELF LOVE/CARE

INTUITIVE MESSAGES

TODAY'S GRATITUDE:

DAILY LOVE WARRIOR CHALLENGE:

Get some art supplies today, markers or colored pencils that you can use in this journal. Plan on doodling, using the line art for coloring book meditations, and getting creative.

DAILY LOVE REFLECTIVE QUESTION:

What do you feel is the current state of your heart?

Empowering

I felt ...

Nurturing

Date:

MORNING MANTRA/PRAYER:

TODAY

05
06
07
08
09
10
11
12
01
02
03
04
05
06
07
08
09
10
11
12

SELF LOVE/CARE

INTUITIVE MESSAGES

TODAY'S GRATITUDE:

DAILY LOVE WARRIOR CHALLENGE:

Take time today to plot out all the dates and special occasions that will be happening for you over these next 12 weeks of the South Direction.

DAILY LOVE REFLECTIVE QUESTION:

What makes you brave?

Empowering

I manifested ...

Nurturing

Date:

TODAY

MORNING MANTRA/PRAYER:

05
06
07
08
09
10
11
12
01
02
03
04
05
06
07
08
09
10
11
12

SELF LOVE/CARE

INTUITIVE MESSAGES

TODAY'S GRATITUDE:

DAILY LOVE WARRIOR CHALLENGE:

Set the intention to work with a spirit teacher for the South Direction, do a meditation to learn and meet this spirit teacher.

DAILY LOVE REFLECTIVE QUESTION:

What areas of your life do you want more vitality?

Empowering

I was inspired by ...

Nurturing

Date:

TODAY

05
06
07
08
09
10
11
12
01
02
03
04
05
06
07
08
09
10
11
12

MORNING MANTRA/PRAYER:

○
○
○
○
○
○
○

○
○
○
○
○
○
○

SELF LOVE/CARE

INTUITIVE MESSAGES

TODAY'S GRATITUDE:

DAILY LOVE WARRIOR CHALLENGE:

Go someplace you can view art—gallery, graffiti in your city, a bookstore—and get inspired by the various colors, shapes, messages, meanings. Take photos (if you are able) of some of the pieces that speak to your heart.

DAILY LOVE REFLECTIVE QUESTION:

How do you express your emotions?

Empowering

I created ...

Nurturing

Date:

TODAY

05 ....
06 ....
07 ....
08 ....
09 ....
10 ....
11 ....
12 ....
01 ....
02 ....
03 ....
04 ....
05 ....
06 ....
07 ....
08 ....
09 ....
10 ....
11 ....
12 ....

MORNING MANTRA/PRAYER:

SELF LOVE/CARE

INTUITIVE MESSAGES

TODAY'S GRATITUDE:

DAILY LOVE WARRIOR CHALLENGE:

Add play to your day—what is your idea of play? How does it make you feel?

DAILY LOVE REFLECTIVE QUESTION:

What types of movement make you feel the most free?

Insights from my

meditation

Suggested Weekly Meditation: ***Manifesting Love*** | www.dakotaearthcloud.com

Date:

Meditation:

Primary Message I Received

I spoke to a tree   and it said to me...

LOOK FOR SIGNS

Throughout the week, be aware of signs, messages, insights that you receive. Log them here.

Aho Mitakuye Oyasin

Becoming our Emotional Genius

This week we focus on our emotional body. It is the primary body for the South Direction. Emotional congruence and intelligence leads us to sustaining healthy relationships with both ourselves, and others. Being able to name our emotions, and feel them fully rather than stuff them, ignore, or let them control us is how we create a healthy homeostasis in our world so that we curb illness and disease.

As kids, we are often not taught how to feel or how to label our emotions and as a result, we lump all feelings into broad buckets. At a certain point, we no longer know who we are or what we are feeling.

"I don't want to be at the mercy of my emotions. I want to use them, to enjoy them, and to dominate them."
Oscar Wilde

My Joys and Loves

Write down all the things which bring you joy or that you love to do or experience. This list will be a wonderful resource when you are planning your soul dates.

Soul Date /sōl/ /dāt/ : An extended period of time you get to spend by yourself, doing something you love. This is a time for you to refuel and replenish your spirit. Spend it solo so you can truly do what you want to do without having to compromise your needs/ wants. Spend the time being fed vs. having to fill someone else's bucket.

1 ....
2 ....
3 ....
4 ....
5 ....
6 ....
7 ....
8 ....
9 ....
10 ....
11 ....
12 ....
13 ....
14 ....
15 ....
16 ....
17 ....
18 ....
19 ....
20 ....
21 ....
22 ....
23 ....
24 ....
25 ....

26 ....
27 ....
28 ....
29 ....
30 ....
31 ....
32 ....
33 ....
34 ....
35 ....
36 ....
37 ....
38 ....
39 ....
40 ....
41 ....
42 ....
43 ....
44 ....
45 ....
46 ....
47 ....
48 ....
49 ....
50 ....

Soul Date Plan:

....

....

....

....

....

Self Love:

....

....

....

....

....

Self Care:

....

....

....

....

....

Relationship to Self

Connect With:

....

....

....

....

....

Nurture:

....

....

....

....

....

Set Boundaries:

....

....

....

....

....

Relationship to Others

Start:

....

....

....

....

....

Continue On:

....

....

....

....

....

Finish:

....

....

....

....

....

Relationship to Goals

WEEKLY OVERVIEW

WORK
GET TO DO LIST

- ○ ....
- ○ ....
- ○ ....
- ○ ....
- ○ ....
- ○ ....

PERSONAL
GET TO DO LIST

- ○ ....
- ○ ....
- ○ ....
- ○ ....
- ○ ....
- ○ ....

SELF-LOVE
GET TO DO LIST

- ○ ....
- ○ ....
- ○ ....
- ○ ....
- ○ ....
- ○ ....

EMOTION CHECK IN

What emotion ruled your day?

- M
- T
- W
- T
- F
- S
- S

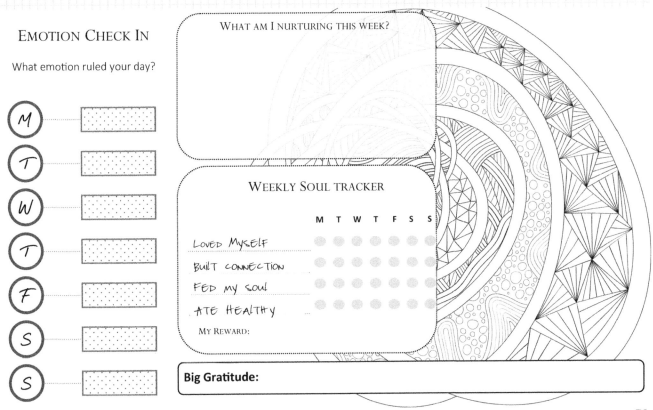

WHAT AM I NURTURING THIS WEEK?

WEEKLY SOUL TRACKER

	M	T	W	T	F	S	S
LOVED MYSELF							
BUILT CONNECTION							
FED MY SOUL							
ATE HEALTHY							

MY REWARD:

Big Gratitude:

Empowering

I am ...

Nurturing

Date:

TODAY

05..
06..
07..
08..
09..
10..
11..
12..
01..
02..
03..
04..
05..
06..
07..
08..
09..
10..
11..
12..

MORNING MANTRA / PRAYER:

○
○
○
○
○
○

○
○
○
○
○
○

SELF LOVE / CARE

INTUITIVE MESSAGES

TODAY'S GRATITUDE:

DAILY LOVE WARRIOR CHALLENGE:

Face one of your fears today. It could be a small fear or a bigger one but make one step towards facing and conquering this fear that has held you back or holds you back from living life

DAILY LOVE REFLECTIVE QUESTION:

How have your fears held you back? What would you do if fear was not facing you?

Empowering

I learned ...

Nurturing

Date:

TODAY

05
06
07
08
09
10
11
12
01
02
03
04
05
06
07
08
09
10
11
12

MORNING MANTRA/PRAYER:

SELF LOVE/CARE

INTUITIVE MESSAGES

TODAY'S GRATITUDE:

DAILY LOVE WARRIOR CHALLENGE:

Keep an emotion log today and record all the various emotions rising up in you at different moments. What precipitated the emotion? Did you allow yourself to feel it fully or did you tamper the emotion down?

DAILY LOVE REFLECTIVE QUESTION:

Which emotions do you tend to cultivate easily?

Empowering

I loved well by ...

Nurturing

Date:

TODAY

MORNING MANTRA/PRAYER:

05 ....
06 ....
07 ....
08 ....
09 ....
10 ....
11 ....
12 ....
01 ....
02 ....
03 ....
04 ....
05 ....
06 ....
07 ....
08 ....
09 ....
10 ....
11 ....
12 ....

SELF LOVE/CARE

INTUITIVE MESSAGES

TODAY'S GRATITUDE:

DAILY LOVE WARRIOR CHALLENGE:

Cultivate a moment of heart-centered love with someone. How did it feel? Did this come easily to you?

DAILY LOVE REFLECTIVE QUESTION:

What emotion is hardest for you to express ? Why?

Empowering

I felt ...

Nurturing

Date:

TODAY

MORNING MANTRA/PRAYER:

05
06
07
08
09
10
11
12
01
02
03
04
05
06
07
08
09
10
11
12

SELF LOVE/CARE

INTUITIVE MESSAGES

TODAY'S GRATITUDE:

DAILY LOVE WARRIOR CHALLENGE:

Look for an opportunity to invoke joy for someone, and ... create a moment of joy for yourself too.

DAILY LOVE REFLECTIVE QUESTION:

What brings you the greatest joy?

Empowering

I manifested ...

Nurturing

Date:

TODAY

05 ....
06 ....
07 ....
08 ....
09 ....
10 ....
11 ....
12 ....
01 ....
02 ....
03 ....
04 ....
05 ....
06 ....
07 ....
08 ....
09 ....
10 ....
11 ....
12 ....

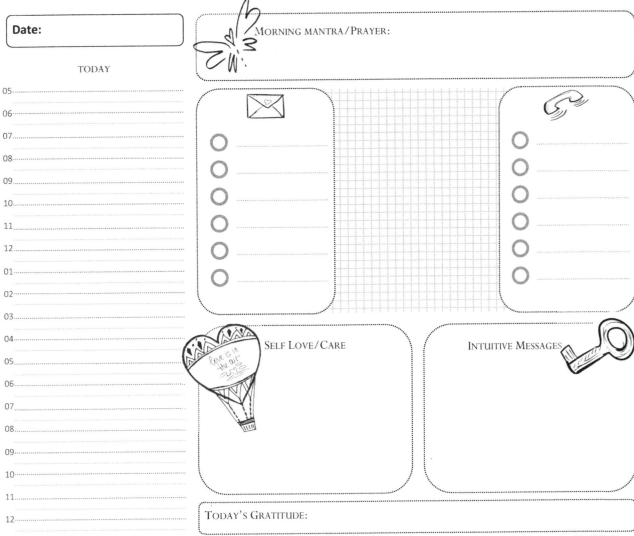

MORNING MANTRA/PRAYER:

SELF LOVE/CARE

INTUITIVE MESSAGES

TODAY'S GRATITUDE:

DAILY LOVE WARRIOR CHALLENGE:

Listen deeply to someone. Ask questions that invoke their story, have a vested interest in them and how they came to be uniquely them.

DAILY LOVE REFLECTIVE QUESTION:

What part of your "story" are you most proud of?

Empowering

I was inspired by ...

Nurturing

Date:

TODAY

05.......................................
06.......................................
07.......................................
08.......................................
09.......................................
10.......................................
11.......................................
12.......................................
01.......................................
02.......................................
03.......................................
04.......................................
05.......................................
06.......................................
07.......................................
08.......................................
09.......................................
10.......................................
11.......................................
12.......................................

MORNING MANTRA/PRAYER:

◯ ....
◯ ....
◯ ....
◯ ....
◯ ....
◯ ....

◯ ....
◯ ....
◯ ....
◯ ....
◯ ....
◯ ....

SELF LOVE/CARE

INTUITIVE MESSAGES

TODAY'S GRATITUDE:

DAILY LOVE WARRIOR CHALLENGE:

Truth telling—tell someone a truth you have not shared or don't share easily, allow yourself to be vulnerable and open.

DAILY LOVE REFLECTIVE QUESTION:

What is the hardest thing for you to share with others? Why?

Empowering

I created ...

Nurturing

Date:

TODAY

MORNING MANTRA/PRAYER:

05..
06..
07..
08..
09..
10..
11..
12..
01..
02..
03..
04..
05..
06..
07..
08..
09..
10..
11..
12..

SELF LOVE/CARE

INTUITIVE MESSAGES

TODAY'S GRATITUDE:

DAILY LOVE WARRIOR CHALLENGE:

Transform your stress today. Choose an activity you can do to lessen or minimize your stress—yoga, meditation, journaling, breathwork .. Whatever it may be.

DAILY LOVE REFLECTIVE QUESTION:

Make a list of activities you feel you would like to try to help minimize stress and overwhelm in your life.

Insights from my meditation

Suggested Weekly Meditation: *Mending Your Emotions* | www.dakotaearthcloud.com

Date:

Meditation:

Primary Message I Received

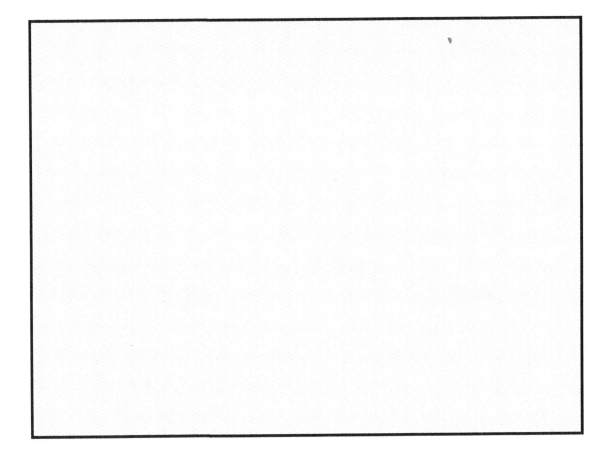

I spoke to a tree   and it said to me...

LOOK FOR SIGNS

Throughout the week, be aware of signs, messages, insights that you receive. Log them here.

Aho Mitakuye Oyasin

WEEKLY CHECK-IN

What I Learned

My Big Wins

My Challenges

Sum Up This Week in 4-5 Words

"But feelings can't be ignored, no matter how unjust or ungrateful they seem."
Anne Frank

Love Thyself

The second core focus of the South Direction is Self-Love. Without it, we are unable to maintain healthy relationships. Most of us have been raised to meet a level of perfectionism to be deemed "good" or "worthy". We then have a measuring stick we are constantly trying to reach, but finding all the reasons we haven't met the standards.

Some of the side effects of constantly straining to reach this imaginary level of perfectionism is a shorter life span. The self-defeating and self-sabotaging effects lead us to illness, disease. Depression, and other adverse affects.

Practicing self-compassion, kindness, love, and understanding are our birthright. We deserve all these building blocks to a healthy and robust life. You have spent years cultivating the inner bully inside you, now it's time to cultivate new tools and build then flex your love muscle.

This week, focus on this South Direction energy and start to nurture new practices to love yourself fully.

"Be proud of who you are, and not ashamed of how someone else sees you.
Above all, be true to yourself, and if you cannot put your heart in it, take yourself out of it
You are allowed to be both a masterpiece and a work in progress simultaneously."

List your good stuff

Write down all your strengths, positive traits, and overall what makes you a great YOU?

Self Love /self/ /ləv/ : Before having any chance at a healthy relationship with someone, you must first nurture the relationship to yourself. Self-love and self-care are paramount foundational skills to building deeply connected, and sacred relationships. Be generous with your love towards yourself!

1 ....
2 ....
3 ....
4 ....
5 ....
6 ....
7 ....
8 ....
9 ....
10 ....
11 ....
12 ....
13 ....
14 ....
15 ....
16 ....
17 ....
18 ....
19 ....
20 ....
21 ....
22 ....
23 ....
24 ....
25 ....

26 ....
27 ....
28 ....
29 ....
30 ....
31 ....
32 ....
33 ....
34 ....
35 ....
36 ....
37 ....
38 ....
39 ....
40 ....
41 ....
42 ....
43 ....
44 ....
45 ....
46 ....
47 ....
48 ....
49 ....
50 ....

Soul Date Plan:

Self Love:

Self Care:

Relationship to Self

Connect With:

Nurture:

Set Boundaries:

Relationship to Others

Start:

Continue On:

Finish:

Relationship to Goals

WEEKLY OVERVIEW

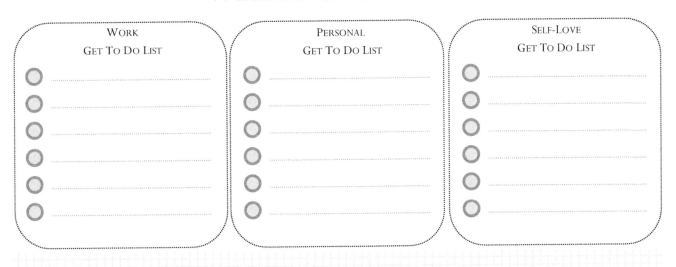

WORK
GET TO DO LIST

○ ....
○ ....
○ ....
○ ....
○ ....
○ ....

PERSONAL
GET TO DO LIST

○ ....
○ ....
○ ....
○ ....
○ ....
○ ....

SELF-LOVE
GET TO DO LIST

○ ....
○ ....
○ ....
○ ....
○ ....
○ ....

EMOTION CHECK IN

What emotion ruled your day?

M
T
W
T
F
S
S

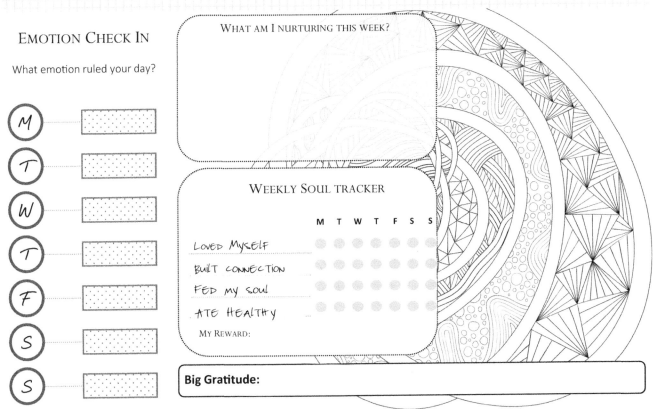

WHAT AM I NURTURING THIS WEEK?

WEEKLY SOUL TRACKER

	M	T	W	T	F	S	S
LOVED MYSELF							
BUILT CONNECTION							
FED MY SOUL							
ATE HEALTHY							

MY REWARD:

Big Gratitude:

Empowering

I am ...

Nurturing

Date:

MORNING MANTRA/PRAYER:

TODAY

05
06
07
08
09
10
11
12
01
02
03
04
05
06
07
08
09
10
11
12

○
○
○
○
○
○

○
○
○
○
○
○

SELF LOVE/CARE

INTUITIVE MESSAGES

TODAY'S GRATITUDE:

DAILY LOVE WARRIOR CHALLENGE:

Choose something from your list of joys and loves from last week and do that today.

DAILY LOVE REFLECTIVE QUESTION:

How do you love your self well on a consistent basis?

Empowering

I learned ...

Nurturing

Date:

TODAY

05 ....
06 ....
07 ....
08 ....
09 ....
10 ....
11 ....
12 ....
01 ....
02 ....
03 ....
04 ....
05 ....
06 ....
07 ....
08 ....
09 ....
10 ....
11 ....
12 ....

MORNING MANTRA / PRAYER:

SELF LOVE / CARE

INTUITIVE MESSAGES

TODAY'S GRATITUDE:

DAILY LOVE WARRIOR CHALLENGE:

Tend to your every need today. If you need rest, then rest. If you need to speak, then speak.

DAILY LOVE REFLECTIVE QUESTION:

What act of self-love do you deny yourself? Why?

113

Empowering

I loved well by ...

Nurturing

Date:

TODAY

MORNING MANTRA / PRAYER:

05 ....
06 ....
07 ....
08 ....
09 ....
10 ....
11 ....
12 ....
01 ....
02 ....
03 ....
04 ....
05 ....
06 ....
07 ....
08 ....
09 ....
10 ....
11 ....
12 ....

SELF LOVE / CARE

INTUITIVE MESSAGES

TODAY'S GRATITUDE:

DAILY LOVE WARRIOR CHALLENGE:

Pay attention to self defeating actions today and rewrite the narrative to empower yourself.

DAILY LOVE REFLECTIVE QUESTION:

What do you love most about yourself?

Empowering

I felt ...

Nurturing

Date:

TODAY

05
06
07
08
09
10
11
12
01
02
03
04
05
06
07
08
09
10
11
12

Morning Mantra/Prayer:

Self Love/Care

Intuitive Messages

Today's Gratitude:

Daily Love Warrior Challenge:

Say yes if you want to say yes, say no if you want to say no. Speak honestly about what you need.

Daily Love reflective question:

What habits do you have that cause you self-harm?

Empowering

I manifested ...

Nurturing

Date:

TODAY

05
06
07
08
09
10
11
12
01
02
03
04
05
06
07
08
09
10
11
12

Morning mantra/Prayer:

Self Love/Care

Intuitive Messages

Today's Gratitude:

Daily Love Warrior Challenge:

Ask someone who you are close with, what they see in you. Ask for the positive and negative and receive with a curious and open heart.

Daily Love reflective question:

What gift do you need the most? Time? Love? Attention?

Empowering

I was inspired by ...

Nurturing

Date:

TODAY

05
06
07
08
09
10
11
12
01
02
03
04
05
06
07
08
09
10
11
12

Morning Mantra / Prayer:

Self Love / Care

Intuitive Messages

Today's Gratitude:

Daily Love Warrior Challenge:

Spend 10 minutes minimum staring into your eyes in a mirror. Create sacred space for this exercise and go as deeply into your soul as you are able. What do you see? Feel?

Daily Love reflective question:

What makes you unique and one of a kind?

Empowering

I created ...

Nurturing

Date:

TODAY

MORNING MANTRA / PRAYER:

05 ....
06 ....
07 ....
08 ....
09 ....
10 ....
11 ....
12 ....
01 ....
02 ....
03 ....
04 ....
05 ....
06 ....
07 ....
08 ....
09 ....
10 ....
11 ....
12 ....

SELF LOVE / CARE

INTUITIVE MESSAGES

TODAY'S GRATITUDE:

DAILY LOVE WARRIOR CHALLENGE:

Choose something healthy today that you might not otherwise normally do. You might drink more water, take the stairs vs the elevator, meditate rather than watch TV. Choose something for the body, mind, and/or soul.

DAILY LOVE REFLECTIVE QUESTION:

What do you need most from you?

Insights from my

meditation

Suggested Weekly Meditation: *Inner Beloved* | www.dakotaearthcloud.com

Date:

Meditation:

Primary Message I Received

I spoke to a tree   and it said to me ...

LOOK FOR SIGNS

Throughout the week, be aware of signs, messages, insights that you receive. Log them here.

Aho Mitakuye Oyasin

WEEKLY CHECK-IN

What I Learned

My Big Wins

My Challenges

Sum Up This Week in 4-5 Words

"Owning our story and loving ourselves through that process is the bravest thing that we'll ever do."
Brene Brown

To be Connected

Our third focus for the South Direction are relationships. We are in relationship at every given moment of the day. We're in relationship with those closest to us—partner, family, friends, co-workers. We are in relationship with the server, the grocery clerk, the banker, and anyone else we come into contact with. We're in relationship with our animals, our space, and with ourselves.

The health of our relationships is dependent on the health of our self-love and compassion and how we care for our own well-being. When we have a poor self-esteem, or feel inadequate, we look outside ourselves for validation, leading to co-dependency. On the contrary, when we have an over inflated ego and see ourselves in comparison to others, we form relationships based on what that person can do for us. These lead to huge imbalances within a relationship, and relationships are built on ego, not spirit.

Relationships are truly the gift of this lifetime. We are tribal by nature, we yearn for connection to others—it's in our DNA. When they are holy, connected, spiritual and sacred, they bring out the very best in us.

"Let us be grateful to the people who make us happy; they are the charming gardeners who make our souls blossom."
Marcel Proust

Ideas for Date Night and Soul Dates

Write down all the ideas you have for a fun, inspiring date with yourself or another (friend, partner, kids, etc.) Use this list and plan your dates!

re·la·tion·ship /rəˈlāSH(ə)nˌSHip/ : the way in which two or more concepts, objects, or people are connected, or the state of being connected. The way in which two or more people or groups regard and behave toward each other. Pay attention to how you are in relationship with those around you—the ones you know, and the ones you don't know

1 ....
2 ....
3 ....
4 ....
5 ....
6 ....
7 ....
8 ....
9 ....
10 ....
11 ....
12 ....
13 ....
14 ....
15 ....
16 ....
17 ....
18 ....
19 ....
20 ....
21 ....
22 ....
23 ....
24 ....
25 ....

26 ....
27 ....
28 ....
29 ....
30 ....
31 ....
32 ....
33 ....
34 ....
35 ....
36 ....
37 ....
38 ....
39 ....
40 ....
41 ....
42 ....
43 ....
44 ....
45 ....
46 ....
47 ....
48 ....
49 ....
50 ....

Soul Date Plan:

....

....

....

....

....

Self Love:

....

....

....

....

....

Self Care:

....

....

....

....

....

Relationship to Self

Connect With:

....

....

....

....

....

Nurture:

....

....

....

....

....

Set Boundaries:

....

....

....

....

....

Relationship to Others

Start:

....

....

....

....

....

Continue On:

....

....

....

....

....

Finish:

....

....

....

....

....

Relationship to Goals

WEEKLY OVERVIEW

WORK
GET TO DO LIST

- ○ ....
- ○ ....
- ○ ....
- ○ ....
- ○ ....
- ○ ....

PERSONAL
GET TO DO LIST

- ○ ....
- ○ ....
- ○ ....
- ○ ....
- ○ ....
- ○ ....

SELF-LOVE
GET TO DO LIST

- ○ ....
- ○ ....
- ○ ....
- ○ ....
- ○ ....
- ○ ....

EMOTION CHECK IN

What emotion ruled your day?

- M
- T
- W
- T
- F
- S
- S

WHAT AM I NURTURING THIS WEEK?

WEEKLY SOUL TRACKER

	M	T	W	T	F	S	S
LOVED MYSELF	●	●	●	●	●	●	
BUILT CONNECTION	●	●	●	●	●	●	
FED MY SOUL	●	●	●	●	●	●	
ATE HEALTHY	●	●	●	●	●	●	

MY REWARD:

Big Gratitude:

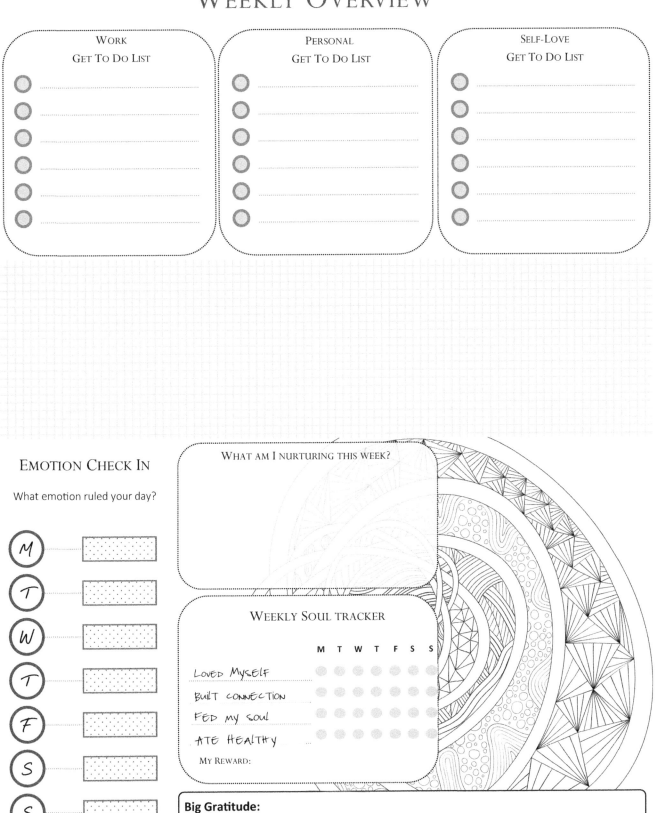

Empowering

I am ...

Nurturing

Date:

TODAY

05
06
07
08
09
10
11
12
01
02
03
04
05
06
07
08
09
10
11
12

MORNING MANTRA / PRAYER:

SELF LOVE / CARE

INTUITIVE MESSAGES

TODAY'S GRATITUDE:

DAILY LOVE WARRIOR CHALLENGE:

Create an act of vulnerability and bravery within one of your relationships today.

DAILY LOVE REFLEC-

What makes a relationship meaningful to you?

Empowering

I learned ...

Nurturing

Date:

TODAY

MORNING MANTRA/PRAYER:

05
06
07
08
09
10
11
12
01
02
03
04
05
06
07
08
09
10
11
12

SELF LOVE/CARE

INTUITIVE MESSAGES

TODAY'S GRATITUDE:

DAILY LOVE WARRIOR CHALLENGE:

Create a moment of connection with someone you have not yet met or have met only briefly.

DAILY LOVE REFLECTIVE QUESTION:

What do you tend to "take on" in your relationships that feels incongruent with your spirit?

143

Empowering

I loved well by ...

Nurturing

Date:

TODAY

MORNING MANTRA/PRAYER:

05
06
07
08
09
10
11
12
01
02
03
04
05
06
07
08
09
10
11
12

SELF LOVE/CARE

INTUITIVE MESSAGES

TODAY'S GRATITUDE:

DAILY LOVE WARRIOR CHALLENGE:

Tell a truth—ask for what you need and/or want in your relationship.

DAILY LOVE REFLECTIVE QUESTION:

What do your current relationships lack that you would like to change or shift?

145

Empowering

I felt ...

Nurturing

Date:

TODAY

05
06
07
08
09
10
11
12
01
02
03
04
05
06
07
08
09
10
11
12

MORNING MANTRA/PRAYER:

SELF LOVE/CARE

INTUITIVE MESSAGES

TODAY'S GRATITUDE:

DAILY LOVE WARRIOR CHALLENGE:

Listen to someone deeply. No need to fix, or advice, or take on—just simply listen with undivided attention and support. Ask questions to help prompt them to go deeper.

DAILY LOVE REFLECTIVE QUESTION:

What do you yearn for?

Empowering

I manifested ...

Nurturing

Date:

TODAY

05
06
07
08
09
10
11
12
01
02
03
04
05
06
07
08
09
10
11
12

MORNING MANTRA/PRAYER:

○
○
○
○
○
○
○

○
○
○
○
○
○

SELF LOVE/CARE

INTUITIVE MESSAGES

TODAY'S GRATITUDE:

DAILY LOVE WARRIOR CHALLENGE:

Create a list of goals you have for your different relationships, take one step towards accomplishing one of your goals.

DAILY LOVE REFLECTIVE QUESTION:

What relationship muscle do you need to strengthen or flex more?

Empowering

I was inspired by ...

Nurturing

Date:

TODAY

MORNING MANTRA/PRAYER:

05

06

07

08

09

10

11

12

01

02

03

04

05

06

07

08

09

10

11

12

SELF LOVE/CARE

INTUITIVE MESSAGES

TODAY'S GRATITUDE:

DAILY LOVE WARRIOR CHALLENGE:

Choose five songs that depict how you feel about someone in your life. Make a playlist or cd, and play the songs for this person.

DAILY LOVE REFLECTIVE QUESTION:

What makes you feel loved and safe?

Empowering

I created ...

Nurturing

Date:

TODAY

05
06
07
08
09
10
11
12
01
02
03
04
05
06
07
08
09
10
11
12

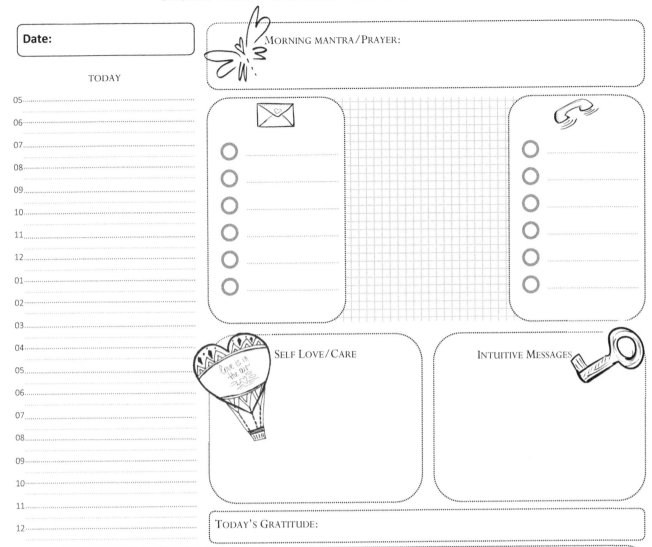

MORNING MANTRA/PRAYER:

SELF LOVE/CARE

INTUITIVE MESSAGES

TODAY'S GRATITUDE:

DAILY LOVE WARRIOR CHALLENGE:

Use your creativity, expertise, love and overall sleuth skills to find out one thing you might not have known about someone close to you. Take it a step further, and surprise them with a gift or experience to show you were listening.

DAILY LOVE REFLECTIVE QUESTION:

What would an ideal date look like?

Insights from my

meditation

Suggested Weekly Meditation: *Loving Unconditionally* | www.dakotaearthcloud.com

Date:

Meditation:

Primary Message I Received

I spoke to a tree *and it said to me...*

LOOK FOR SIGNS

Throughout the week, be aware of signs, messages, insights that you receive. Log them here.

Aho Mitakuye Oyasin

Weekly Check-In

What I Learned

My Big Wins

My Challenges

Sum Up This Week in 4-5 Words

"The most important thing in life is to learn how to give out love, and to let it come in."
Domenico Cieri Estrada

Coming Alive

Vibrancy. Feeling ALIVE. Energy. Creativity. Joy. Laughter. These are the undercurrents of the South Direction. It brings us to life and reminds of what it feels like to be so fully present, and connected. These are the seeds we nurture that will fuel us in all the moments of our life.

We have to unearth what brings us to life. Sometimes the seeds are buried deep and have been long forgotten. We have forgotten how to play, or we stop ourselves short of uncontrollable belly laughing. We take life far too seriously and get caught up in the mundane, the overwhelming schedule, the responsibilities.

So this week, come undone in a good way. Dance, laugh, do all the things you have denied yourself for far too long. Cut yourself loose!

"Dance. Smile. Giggle. Marvel. TRUST. HOPE. LOVE. WISH. BELIEVE. Most of all, enjoy every moment of the journey, and appreciate where you are at this moment instead of always focusing on how far you have to go."
—Mandy Hale

5

Things that make me come alive

Write down all the things that make you come alive.

Play Tip: Participate in laughter yoga. Create a playlist of music that makes you move. Get sidewalk chalk and draw yourself on the sidewalk or driveway. Host a play party for you and your friends. Make a blanket fort and watch old movies. Sing loudly with the windows rolled down. Get creative ...

1 ....
2 ....
3 ....
4 ....
5 ....
6 ....
7 ....
8 ....
9 ....
10 ....
11 ....
12 ....
13 ....
14 ....
15 ....
16 ....
17 ....
18 ....
19 ....
20 ....
21 ....
22 ....
23 ....
24 ....
25 ....

26 ....
27 ....
28 ....
29 ....
30 ....
31 ....
32 ....
33 ....
34 ....
35 ....
36 ....
37 ....
38 ....
39 ....
40 ....
41 ....
42 ....
43 ....
44 ....
45 ....
46 ....
47 ....
48 ....
49 ....
50 ....

Soul Date Plan:

....
....
....
....
....

Self Love:

....
....
....
....
....

Self Care:

....
....
....
....
....

Relationship to Self

Connect With:

....
....
....
....
....

Nurture:

....
....
....
....
....

Set Boundaries:

....
....
....
....
....

Relationship to Others

Start:

....
....
....
....
....

Continue On:

....
....
....
....
....

Finish:

....
....
....
....
....

Relationship to Goals

WEEKLY OVERVIEW

WORK
GET TO DO LIST

PERSONAL
GET TO DO LIST

SELF-LOVE
GET TO DO LIST

EMOTION CHECK IN

What emotion ruled your day?

M

T

W

T

F

S

S

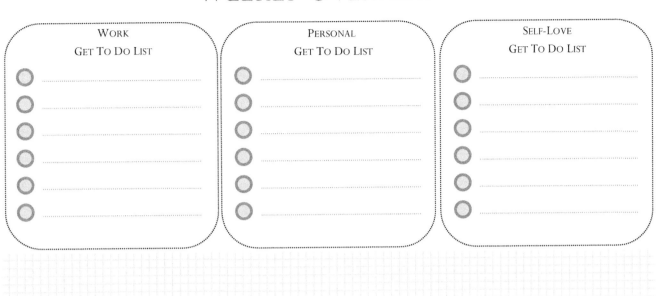

WHAT AM I NURTURING THIS WEEK?

WEEKLY SOUL TRACKER

	M	T	W	T	F	S	S
LOVED MYSELF							
BUILT CONNECTION							
FED MY SOUL							
ATE HEALTHY							

MY REWARD:

Big Gratitude:

Empowering

I am ...

Nurturing

Date:

TODAY

MORNING MANTRA/PRAYER:

05
06
07
08
09
10
11
12
01
02
03
04
05
06
07
08
09
10
11
12

SELF LOVE/CARE

INTUITIVE MESSAGES

TODAY'S GRATITUDE:

DAILY LOVE WARRIOR CHALLENGE:

Do something that terrifies you. Face the fear, and do it anyway.

DAILY LOVE REFLECTIVE QUESTION:

What makes you come alive?

Empowering

I learned ...

Nurturing

Date:

TODAY

05
06
07
08
09
10
11
12
01
02
03
04
05
06
07
08
09
10
11
12

MORNING MANTRA/PRAYER:

SELF LOVE/CARE

INTUITIVE MESSAGES

TODAY'S GRATITUDE:

DAILY LOVE WARRIOR CHALLENGE:

Induce a fit of laughter—watch a comedy, do laughter yoga, or simply start laughing until it "catches".

DAILY LOVE REFLECTIVE QUESTION:

Describe the untapped passion within you.

Empowering

I loved well by ...

Nurturing

Date:

TODAY

05
06
07
08
09
10
11
12
01
02
03
04
05
06
07
08
09
10
11
12

MORNING MANTRA/PRAYER:

SELF LOVE/CARE

INTUITIVE MESSAGES

TODAY'S GRATITUDE:

DAILY LOVE WARRIOR CHALLENGE:

Break the pattern ... do something wild and unpredictable!

DAILY LOVE REFLECTIVE QUESTION:

If you could do anything without fear or regret, what would you do? What stops you?

Empowering

I felt ...

Nurturing

Date:

TODAY

MORNING MANTRA/PRAYER:

05..
06..
07..
08..
09..
10..
11..
12..
01..
02..
03..
04..
05..
06..
07..
08..
09..
10..
11..
12..

SELF LOVE/CARE

INTUITIVE MESSAGES

TODAY'S GRATITUDE:

DAILY LOVE WARRIOR CHALLENGE:

Stand up for yourself, or champion and be your own cheerleader!

DAILY LOVE REFLECTIVE QUESTION:

What do you commonly deny yourself that you secretly wish you could do or have?

Empowering

I manifested ...

Nurturing

Date:

TODAY

MORNING MANTRA/PRAYER:

05

06

07

08

09

10

11

12

01

02

03

04

SELF LOVE/CARE

INTUITIVE MESSAGES

05

06

07

08

09

10

11

12

TODAY'S GRATITUDE:

DAILY LOVE WARRIOR CHALLENGE:

Finish something you have been procrastinating.

DAILY LOVE REFLECTIVE QUESTION:

What old pattern (s) do you have that stifles you?

Empowering

I was inspired by ...

Nurturing

Date:

TODAY

05
06
07
08
09
10
11
12
01
02
03
04
05
06
07
08
09
10
11
12

MORNING MANTRA/PRAYER:

SELF LOVE/CARE

INTUITIVE MESSAGES

TODAY'S GRATITUDE:

DAILY LOVE WARRIOR CHALLENGE:

Move, dance, exercise ... do something that moves multiple muscles in your body for a minimum of 20 minutes!

DAILY LOVE REFLECTIVE QUESTION:

We all have a secret hidden self, what do you hide?

Empowering

I created ...

Nurturing

Date:

TODAY

MORNING MANTRA/PRAYER:

05
06
07
08
09
10
11
12
01
02
03
04
05
06
07
08
09
10
11
12

SELF LOVE/CARE

INTUITIVE MESSAGES

TODAY'S GRATITUDE:

DAILY LOVE WARRIOR CHALLENGE:

Gather up your art supplies, paint, draw or sculpt your soul. Pro Tip: add a playlist to your event—songs that move you, inspire you, reflect you ...

DAILY LOVE REFLECTIVE QUESTION:

What holds you back from living full out?

Insights from my

meditation

Suggested Weekly Meditation: *Ignite Your Inner Fire* | www.dakotaearthcloud.com

Date:

Meditation:

Primary Message I Received

I spoke to a tree   and it said to me...

LOOK FOR SIGNS

Throughout the week, be aware of signs, messages, insights that you receive. Log them here.

Aho Mitakuye Oyasin

WEEKLY CHECK-IN

What I Learned

My Big Wins

My Challenges

Sum Up This Week in 4-5 Words

"All life is an experiment. The more experiments you make the better."
Ralph Waldo Emerson

Twin Flames, Soul Mates, and our Sacred Feminine/Divine Masculine

We are connected to our spiritual bodies through threads of being and access to our divinity is more easily obtained when are balanced between our Sacred Feminine and Divine Masculine. To offer this duality a shared space in our lives creates a more expansive vision for who we are at a soul level. We are not defined by the gender of the body we have chosen to be our host in this lifetime, we are not limited by they physical when we embrace and utilize the power of both.

We are also more aligned with our truth when surrounded by our Soul Family and Soul Mates. These are the souls we have travelled with over thousands of years. And then there is the other half of you ... your Twin Flame, the part of you that split at the beginning of your soul's incarnation. Building and forging this relationship will altar your purpose drastically. When twin flames come together, it is specifically to create a masterpiece in this lifetime. It is both a haunting and transformational experience. The level and depth of love is unmatched by anything else in the world.

"Our souls already know each other, don't they?' he whispered. 'It's our bodies that are new."
Karen Ross

Ways I feel or find connection

Write down all the things that create a moment of connection for you— whether to nature, yourself, spirit, or others.

Soul Tip: Create sacred space prior to meditating or doing soul work. This invites in positive energies and sets the stage for more meaningful connection to the energies you wish to connect with. Likewise, do the same if you are in nature or doing something active outside—set intentions, eat healthy, drink water, and leave distractions behind.

1 ....
2 ....
3 ....
4 ....
5 ....
6 ....
7 ....
8 ....
9 ....
10 ....
11 ....
12 ....
13 ....
14 ....
15 ....
16 ....
17 ....
18 ....
19 ....
20 ....
21 ....
22 ....
23 ....
24 ....
25 ....

26 ....
27 ....
28 ....
29 ....
30 ....
31 ....
32 ....
33 ....
34 ....
35 ....
36 ....
37 ....
38 ....
39 ....
40 ....
41 ....
42 ....
43 ....
44 ....
45 ....
46 ....
47 ....
48 ....
49 ....
50 ....

Soul Date Plan:

Self Love:

Self Care:

....

....

....

....

....

Relationship to Self

Connect With:

Nurture:

Set Boundaries:

....

....

....

....

....

Relationship to Others

Start:

Continue On:

Finish:

....

....

....

....

....

Relationship to Goals

WEEKLY OVERVIEW

WORK
GET TO DO LIST

PERSONAL
GET TO DO LIST

SELF-LOVE
GET TO DO LIST

EMOTION CHECK IN

What emotion ruled your day?

M

T

W

T

F

S

S

WHAT AM I NURTURING THIS WEEK?

WEEKLY SOUL TRACKER

	M	T	W	T	F	S	S
LOVED MYSELF							
BUILT CONNECTION							
FED MY SOUL							
ATE HEALTHY							

MY REWARD:

Big Gratitude:

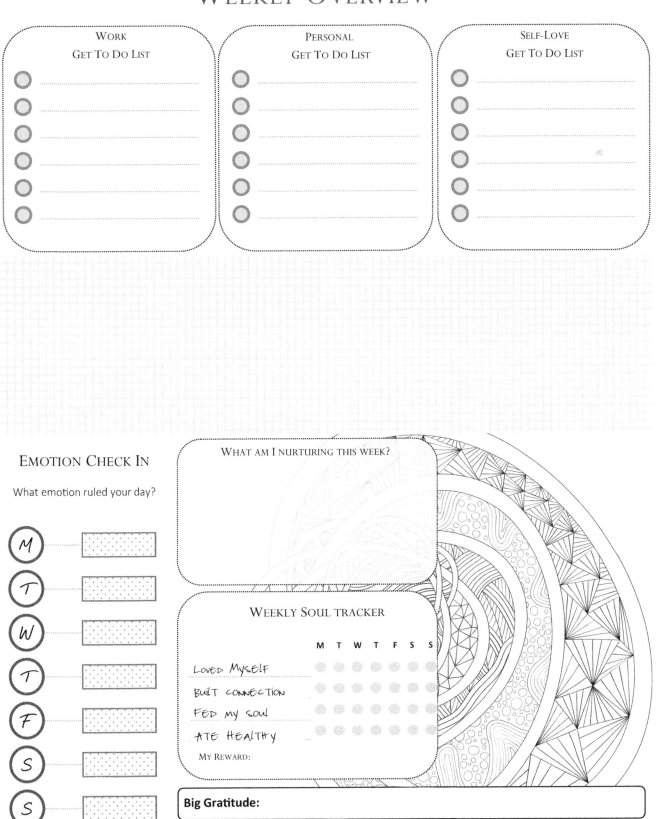

Empowering

I am ...

Nurturing

Date:

TODAY

05
06
07
08
09
10
11
12
01
02
03
04
05
06
07
08
09
10
11
12

MORNING MANTRA/PRAYER:

SELF LOVE/CARE

INTUITIVE MESSAGES

TODAY'S GRATITUDE:

DAILY LOVE WARRIOR CHALLENGE:

For the day, exaggerate the feminine side of you.

DAILY LOVE REFLECTIVE QUESTION:

Describe the divine feminine within you ...

Empowering

I learned ...

Nurturing

Date:

TODAY

05
06
07
08
09
10
11
12
01
02
03
04
05
06
07
08
09
10
11
12

MORNING MANTRA/PRAYER:

SELF LOVE/CARE

INTUITIVE MESSAGES

TODAY'S GRATITUDE:

DAILY LOVE WARRIOR CHALLENGE:

For the day, exaggerate the masculine side of you.

DAILY LOVE REFLECTIVE QUESTION:

Describe the sacred masculine within you ...

Empowering

I loved well by ...

Nurturing

Date:

TODAY

MORNING MANTRA/PRAYER:

05
06
07
08
09
10
11
12
01
02
03
04
05
06
07
08
09
10
11
12

SELF LOVE/CARE

INTUITIVE MESSAGES

TODAY'S GRATITUDE:

DAILY LOVE WARRIOR CHALLENGE:

Look for signs of your twin flame today. What messages did you receive from them?

DAILY LOVE REFLECTIVE QUESTION:

How does your connection to your twin flame or soul mate change you?

Empowering

I felt ...

Nurturing

Date:

TODAY

05
06
07
08
09
10
11
12
01
02
03
04
05
06
07
08
09
10
11
12

MORNING MANTRA/PRAYER:

SELF LOVE/CARE

INTUITIVE MESSAGES

TODAY'S GRATITUDE:

DAILY LOVE WARRIOR CHALLENGE:

Create a ritual for you to connect with your twin flame and/or soul mate.

DAILY LOVE REFLECTIVE QUESTION:

Describe the fire inside your belly.

Empowering

I manifested ...

Nurturing

Date:

TODAY

MORNING MANTRA/PRAYER:

05 ....
06 ....
07 ....
08 ....
09 ....
10 ....
11 ....
12 ....
01 ....
02 ....
03 ....
04 ....
05 ....
06 ....
07 ....
08 ....
09 ....
10 ....
11 ....
12 ....

SELF LOVE/CARE

INTUITIVE MESSAGES

TODAY'S GRATITUDE:

DAILY LOVE WARRIOR CHALLENGE:

Write a love letter to your twin flame, or your soul mate, or to the inner divine within you (or to all 3!).

DAILY LOVE REFLECTIVE QUESTION:

Tap into your twin flame, what are the two of you inspired to create in this lifetime?

Empowering

I was inspired by ...

Nurturing

Date:

TODAY

MORNING MANTRA/PRAYER:

05

06

07

08

09

10

11

12

01

02

03

04

SELF LOVE/CARE

INTUITIVE MESSAGES

05

06

07

08

09

10

11

12

TODAY'S GRATITUDE:

DAILY LOVE WARRIOR CHALLENGE:

Spend the day collecting "talismans" for your twin flame or soul mate. Collect items from nature, or random items that symbolize the connection you have with them. If you can't give them to your connected one, then put them in a special container on your altar.

DAILY LOVE REFLECTIVE QUESTION:

What do you ache for?

Empowering

I created ...

Nurturing

Date:

TODAY

MORNING MANTRA/PRAYER:

05
06
07
08
09
10
11
12
01
02
03
04
05
06
07
08
09
10
11
12

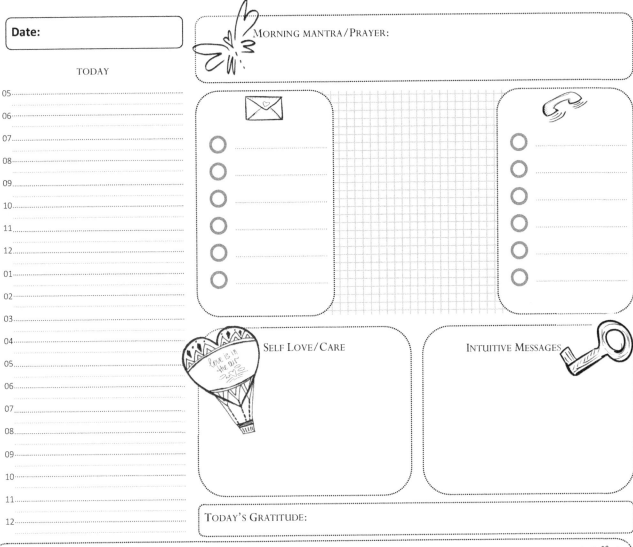

SELF LOVE/CARE

INTUITIVE MESSAGES

TODAY'S GRATITUDE:

DAILY LOVE WARRIOR CHALLENGE:

Take any opportunity you can today to find a way to balance the feminine and masculine sides of yourself.

DAILY LOVE REFLECTIVE QUESTION:

How can you balance the masculine and feminine sides more?

Insights from my meditation

Suggested Weekly Meditation: *Journey of a Thousand Lifetimes* | www.dakotaearthcloud.com

Date:

Meditation:

Primary Message I Received

I spoke to a tree   and it said to me...

LOOK FOR SIGNS

Throughout the week, be aware of signs, messages, insights that you receive. Log them here.

Aho Mitakuye Oyasin

WEEKLY CHECK-IN

What I Learned

My Big Wins

My Challenges

Sum Up This Week in 4-5 Words

"You have half our gifts. I the other. Together we make a whole. Together we are much more powerful."
Joss Stirling

Sensing the World Around You

Our sensory system is one of the gateways that our Spirit Guides use to communicate with us. In the past, we've been led to believe we have 5-7 senses but more recently, it science is claiming we have upwards to 20 senses. The most basic definition of a sense is it is a channel through which your body can observe itself or the outside world. The more we can open these sensory channels, the easier our Spirit Guides can communicate and we can receive messages.

Some of the other senses we have that may be new to you:

Proprioception: You can close your eyes, life a finger to touch your head and you know exactly where it is without looking. That's proprioception.

Equilibrioception: This is your sense of balance. If you remember twirling yourself as a kid, you know how disorientating this sense can become when you fall down and attempt to get back up.

Magnetoreception is our ability to detect magnetic fields around us whereas **electroception** is sensing electrical fields.

Expanding on those last two, consider this: thoughts are electrical while emotions are magnetic.

Spend this week playing with your senses and honing in on where your strengths are and which senses you could use opening more.

"Memories establish the past; Senses perceive the present; Imaginations shape the future."
Toba Beta

Things I love
to see, smell, taste, feel, hear.

Write down all the things that tantalize your senses and make you feel awesome! Once written, look through list and see if there is a dominant sense that stands out to you.

Soul Tip: Want to heighten your senses even more? Try this: commit to wearing a blindfold for 2-8 hours and focus on all your other senses. Which sense is most dominant without sight? You can do the same by wearing noise cancelling headphones to muffle sound. Taking away a dominant sense helps to open the others.

1 ....
2 ....
3 ....
4 ....
5 ....
6 ....
7 ....
8 ....
9 ....
10 ....
11 ....
12 ....
13 ....
14 ....
15 ....
16 ....
17 ....
18 ....
19 ....
20 ....
21 ....
22 ....
23 ....
24 ....
25 ....

26 ....
27 ....
28 ....
29 ....
30 ....
31 ....
32 ....
33 ....
34 ....
35 ....
36 ....
37 ....
38 ....
39 ....
40 ....
41 ....
42 ....
43 ....
44 ....
45 ....
46 ....
47 ....
48 ....
49 ....
50 ....

Soul Date Plan:

Self Love:

Self Care:

Relationship to Self

Connect With:

Nurture:

Set Boundaries:

Relationship to Others

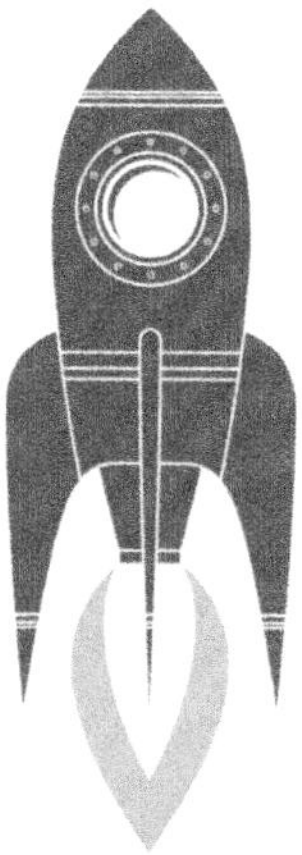

Start:

Continue On:

Finish:

Relationship to Goals

WEEKLY OVERVIEW

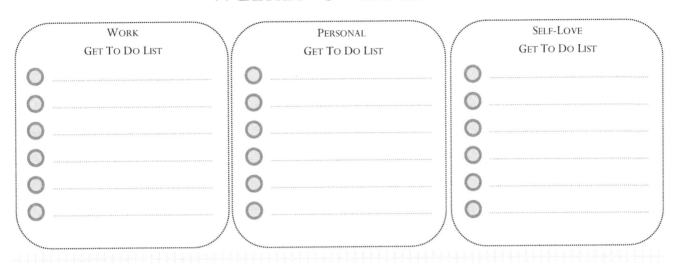

WORK
GET TO DO LIST

PERSONAL
GET TO DO LIST

SELF-LOVE
GET TO DO LIST

EMOTION CHECK IN

What emotion ruled your day?

- M
- T
- W
- T
- F
- S
- S

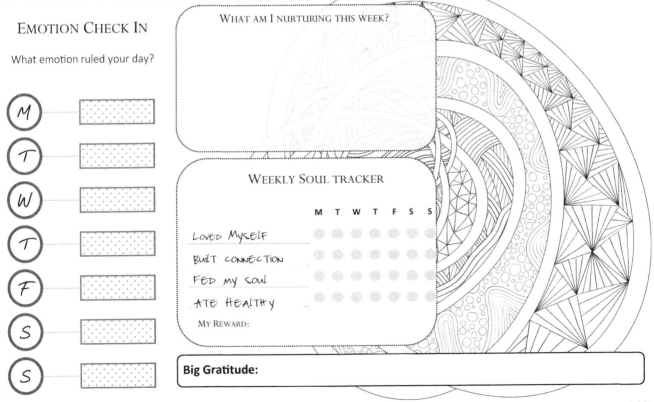

WHAT AM I NURTURING THIS WEEK?

WEEKLY SOUL TRACKER

	M	T	W	T	F	S	S
LOVED MYSELF							
BUILT CONNECTION							
FED MY SOUL							
ATE HEALTHY							

MY REWARD:

Big Gratitude:

Empowering

I am ...

Nurturing

Date:

TODAY

05
06
07
08
09
10
11
12
01
02
03
04
05
06
07
08
09
10
11
12

MORNING MANTRA/PRAYER:

SELF LOVE/CARE

INTUITIVE MESSAGES

TODAY'S GRATITUDE:

DAILY LOVE WARRIOR CHALLENGE:

Focus on your sense of smell today. Smell everything, go out of your way to fill your space with aroma. Play with different smells, see how a woodsy smell invokes a different feeling vs. an aroma that is more floral, or soft. And don't be afraid of the aromas that aren't so delightful!

DAILY LOVE REFLECTIVE QUESTION:

Describe the most resplendent smell you have ever smelled. What does that scent invoke for you or remind you of?

Empowering

I learned ...

Nurturing

Date:

TODAY

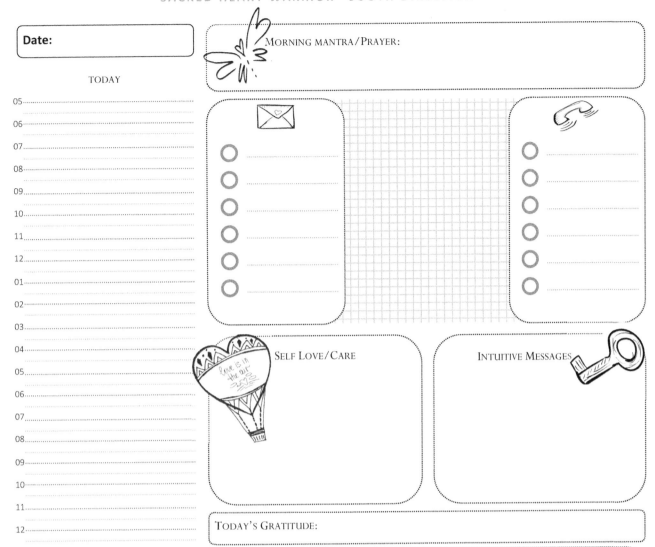

MORNING MANTRA/PRAYER:

05

06

07

08

09

10

11

12

01

02

03

04

05

06

07

08

09

10

11

12

SELF LOVE/CARE

INTUITIVE MESSAGES

TODAY'S GRATITUDE:

DAILY LOVE WARRIOR CHALLENGE:

Focus on your sense of touch today. Touch as many things as you can with as varied textures as you can. What did you notice? What felt the nicest? What made you squirm? Go out of your way to try out different textures and experiences.

DAILY LOVE REFLECTIVE QUESTION:

How do you experience the world most often?

Empowering

I loved well by ...

Nurturing

Date:

MORNING MANTRA/PRAYER:

TODAY

05
06
07
08
09
10
11
12
01
02
03
04
05
06
07
08
09
10
11
12

○
○
○
○
○
○
○

○
○
○
○
○
○
○

SELF LOVE/CARE

INTUITIVE MESSAGES

TODAY'S GRATITUDE:

DAILY LOVE WARRIOR CHALLENGE:

Focus on your sense of sound today. Close your eyes and try to pick out the tiniest of sounds. Take notice of how the sounds evoke different responses/emotions within you.

DAILY LOVE REFLECTIVE QUESTION:

What sounds bring you the most sense of peace?

Empowering

I felt ...

Nurturing

Date:

TODAY

05
06
07
08
09
10
11
12
01
02
03
04
05
06
07
08
09
10
11
12

MORNING MANTRA/PRAYER:

○
○
○
○
○
○
○

○
○
○
○
○
○
○

SELF LOVE/CARE

INTUITIVE MESSAGES

TODAY'S GRATITUDE:

DAILY LOVE WARRIOR CHALLENGE:

Focus on your sense of taste today. Within reason, try a variety of tastes. Do any invoke memories or feelings within you? What tastes satisfy you most?

DAILY LOVE REFLECTIVE QUESTION:

Which sense do you rely on most when tapping into your intuition?

237

Empowering

I manifested ...

Nurturing

Date:

TODAY

05
06
07
08
09
10
11
12
01
02
03
04
05
06
07
08
09
10
11
12

MORNING MANTRA/PRAYER:

SELF LOVE/CARE

INTUITIVE MESSAGES

TODAY'S GRATITUDE:

DAILY LOVE WARRIOR CHALLENGE:

Focus on your sense of sight today. Pay attention to what draws your attention. What draws you in the most? Spend time looking beyond what you are looking at and looking for the hidden symbols or meaning.

DAILY LOVE REFLECTIVE QUESTION:

What is the most beautiful thing you have ever seen? How did it move you or change you?

Empowering

I was inspired by ...

Nurturing

Date:

TODAY

MORNING MANTRA/PRAYER:

05
06
07
08
09
10
11
12
01
02
03
04
05
06
07
08
09
10
11
12

SELF LOVE/CARE

INTUITIVE MESSAGES

TODAY'S GRATITUDE:

DAILY LOVE WARRIOR CHALLENGE:

Using all your senses today, plug into a moment in real time and use all of your senses to gather information about the event. Record your findings.

DAILY LOVE REFLECTIVE QUESTION:

When meeting someone new, which sense do you activate first? The sound of their voice? The way they look? How their energy feels? How does this

Empowering

I created ...

Nurturing

Date:

TODAY

05
06
07
08
09
10
11
12
01
02
03
04
05
06
07
08
09
10
11
12

MORNING MANTRA/PRAYER:

SELF LOVE/CARE

INTUITIVE MESSAGES

TODAY'S GRATITUDE:

DAILY LOVE WARRIOR CHALLENGE:

Today, play with your sense of perception and spatial orientation. Notice where you land in a crowd, or how space feels differently in different places. Move around, experience the space in as many different places as you can.

DAILY LOVE REFLECTIVE QUESTION:

Which sense do you rely on the most? Why?

Insights from my

meditation

Suggested Weekly Meditation: *Unfolding the Senses* | www.dakotaearthcloud.com

Date:

Meditation:

Primary Message I Received

LOOK FOR SIGNS

Throughout the week, be aware of signs, messages, insights that you receive. Log them here.

Aho Mitakuye Oyasin

WEEKLY CHECK-IN

What I Learned

My Big Wins

My Challenges

Sum Up This Week in 4-5 Words

"Senses empower limitations, senses expand vision within borders, senses promote understanding through pleasure." Dejan Stojanovic

Listening Inward

Our other core foundation for the South Direction is Intuition and Empathy. Along with our sensory system, the intuitive system is another avenue our Spirit Guides use for communicating with us.

Intuition is also crucial for combing with the East Energy of the mental body so we are making choices for our life with both our gut and our head. If you have excess energy in the South, you must learn how to balance the intuition with your mental body. If you have deficient energy in the South, you'll need to learn how to lean into your intuition more and how to trust yourself.

Along with intuition, is empathy—the ability to understand or share what others are feeling or experiencing. Our empathy muscle is what helps us to create sacred relationship. Without it, connecting with others simply won't happen. If you have excess South energy, your empathy muscle may be too open with no boundaries and you take on the energy of everything, leading to exhaustion, illness, and suppressed emotions. If you have deficient South energy, your empathy muscle is atrophied leading to shallow relationships.

It is worth continuing this work past one week, for sure. Building both these muscles should be a daily "get-to".

"I believe in intuitions and inspirations...I sometimes FEEL that I am right. I do not KNOW that I am."
Albert Einstein

8

Messages I've received this week

Write down all the symbols, messages, intuitive feelings, and more that you receive this week.

Soul Tip : Carry a small notebook with you so you can write down any messages, ideas, gut feelings, and more. Your Spirit Guides are talking to you constantly, it's hard to remember every single message in one day. Writing them down allows you to capture them all but also to see them in context of the bigger picture.

1 ....
2 ....
3 ....
4 ....
5 ....
6 ....
7 ....
8 ....
9 ....
10 ....
11 ....
12 ....
13 ....
14 ....
15 ....
16 ....
17 ....
18 ....
19 ....
20 ....
21 ....
22 ....
23 ....
24 ....
25 ....

26 ....
27 ....
28 ....
29 ....
30 ....
31 ....
32 ....
33 ....
34 ....
35 ....
36 ....
37 ....
38 ....
39 ....
40 ....
41 ....
42 ....
43 ....
44 ....
45 ....
46 ....
47 ....
48 ....
49 ....
50 ....

Soul Date Plan:

Self Love:

Self Care:

....

....

....

....

....

Relationship to Self

Connect With:

Nurture:

Set Boundaries:

....

....

....

....

....

Relationship to Others

Start:

Continue On:

Finish:

....

....

....

....

....

Relationship to Goals

WEEKLY OVERVIEW

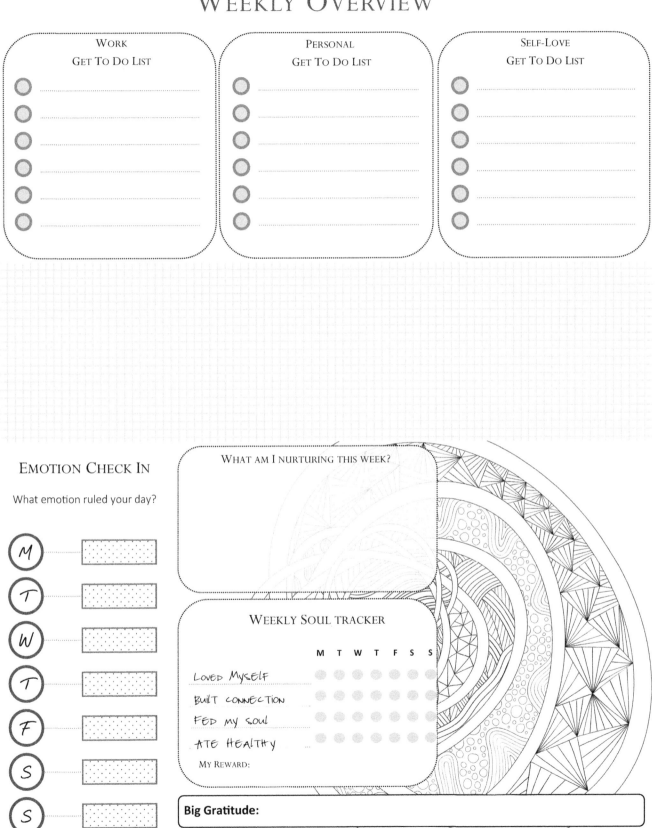

WORK
GET TO DO LIST

PERSONAL
GET TO DO LIST

SELF-LOVE
GET TO DO LIST

EMOTION CHECK IN

What emotion ruled your day?

M

T

W

T

F

S

S

WHAT AM I NURTURING THIS WEEK?

WEEKLY SOUL TRACKER

	M	T	W	T	F	S	S
LOVED MYSELF							
BUILT CONNECTION							
FED MY SOUL							
ATE HEALTHY							

MY REWARD:

Big Gratitude:

Empowering

I am ...

Nurturing

Date:

TODAY

05
06
07
08
09
10
11
12
01
02
03
04
05
06
07
08
09
10
11
12

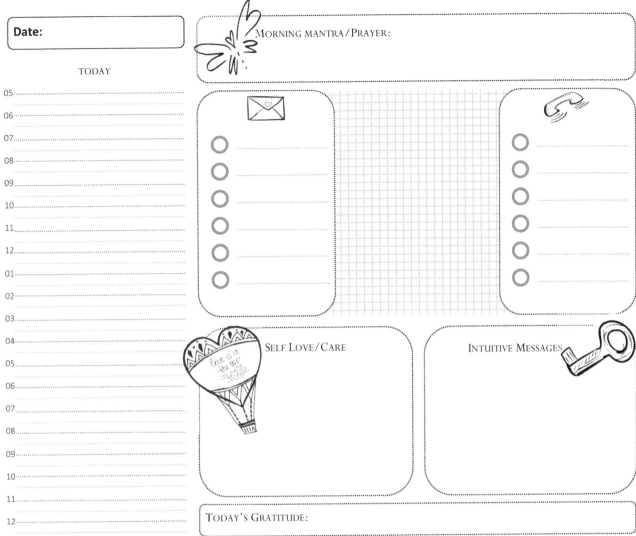

MORNING MANTRA / PRAYER:

SELF LOVE / CARE

INTUITIVE MESSAGES

TODAY'S GRATITUDE:

DAILY LOVE WARRIOR CHALLENGE:

Through your eyes—Today, take photos of anything that catches your attention. At the end of the day, compile your photos together to see what "story" they tell you. Is there a theme? Does it answer a question that has been lingering for you?

DAILY LOVE REFLECTIVE QUESTION:

Where do you feel you receive the most signs? Nature? Everyday life? People? How do these speak to you?

Empowering

I learned ...

Nurturing

Date:

TODAY

05
06
07
08
09
10
11
12
01
02
03
04
05
06
07
08
09
10
11
12

MORNING MANTRA/PRAYER:

SELF LOVE/CARE

INTUITIVE MESSAGES

TODAY'S GRATITUDE:

DAILY LOVE WARRIOR CHALLENGE:

Randomly pick up various books which appear in your path. It might be a book left on a table, or a book from your own library. Open each one to page 33. At first glance, write down the first few words your eyes land on. Sew your findings together into a poem or story. What does it tell you?

DAILY LOVE REFLECTIVE QUESTION:

What question do you most want answered?

Empowering

I loved well by ...

Nurturing

Date:

TODAY

MORNING MANTRA/PRAYER:

05
06
07
08
09
10
11
12
01
02
03
04
05
06
07
08
09
10
11
12

SELF LOVE/CARE

INTUITIVE MESSAGES

TODAY'S GRATITUDE:

DAILY LOVE WARRIOR CHALLENGE:

Find something in nature that you can spend time exploring closely. Look at the micro details, the colors, patterns, how it is in relationship to the other things around it How do you represent this piece of nature? What message does it speak to you?

DAILY LOVE REFLECTIVE QUESTION:

Right now, write down anything that comes to your mind.

Empowering

I felt ...

Nurturing

Date:

TODAY

05
06
07
08
09
10
11
12
01
02
03
04
05
06
07
08
09
10
11
12

MORNING MANTRA/PRAYER:

○
○
○
○
○
○

○
○
○
○
○
○

SELF LOVE/CARE

INTUITIVE MESSAGES

TODAY'S GRATITUDE:

DAILY LOVE WARRIOR CHALLENGE:

Pay attention to which animals appear in your day. Did you see this animal more than once? Tap into the energy of the animal, what is its message to you? What medicine does it offer you?

DAILY LOVE REFLECTIVE QUESTION:

From the perspective of an animal, answer this question: What I need most right now is ...

Empowering

I manifested ...

Nurturing

Date:

TODAY

05 ....
06 ....
07 ....
08 ....
09 ....
10 ....
11 ....
12 ....
01 ....
02 ....
03 ....
04 ....
05 ....
06 ....
07 ....
08 ....
09 ....
10 ....
11 ....
12 ....

MORNING MANTRA/PRAYER:

○
○
○
○
○
○

○
○
○
○
○
○

SELF LOVE/CARE

INTUITIVE MESSAGES

TODAY'S GRATITUDE:

DAILY LOVE WARRIOR CHALLENGE:

Using your non-dominant hand, write a letter to yourself from your higher self.

DAILY LOVE REFLECTIVE QUESTION:

What keeps you from trusting your intuition?

Empowering

I was inspired by ...

Nurturing

Date:

TODAY

MORNING MANTRA/PRAYER:

05
06
07
08
09
10
11
12
01
02
03
04
05
06
07
08
09
10
11
12

SELF LOVE/CARE

INTUITIVE MESSAGES

TODAY'S GRATITUDE:

DAILY LOVE WARRIOR CHALLENGE:

Choose 3 oracle cards, one for past, present and future. Give yourself a reading without using a book to interpret the cards. Interpret them instead using your imagination, the symbols, colors, and anything else that strikes you.

DAILY LOVE REFLECTIVE QUESTION:

Which chakra feels the strongest for you? Weakest?

Empowering

I created ...

Nurturing

Date:

TODAY

05
06
07
08
09
10
11
12
01
02
03
04
05
06
07
08
09
10
11
12

MORNING MANTRA/PRAYER:

SELF LOVE/CARE

INTUITIVE MESSAGES

TODAY'S GRATITUDE:

DAILY LOVE WARRIOR CHALLENGE:

Using a photo from your past, consciously enter into the scene and experience the event as an observer from the future. What do you notice?

DAILY LOVE REFLECTIVE QUESTION:

What clutter do you need to clear away in your life so you can listen more clearly to your intuition?

Insights from my
meditation

Suggested Weekly Meditation: *Fire in the Belly* | www.dakotaearthcloud.com

Date:

Meditation:

Primary Message I Received

I spoke to a tree   *and it said to me ...*

LOOK FOR SIGNS

Throughout the week, be aware of signs, messages, insights that you receive. Log them here.

Aho Mitakuye Oyasin

WEEKLY CHECK-IN

What I Learned

My Big Wins

My Challenges

Sum Up This Week in 4-5 Words

"Don't try to comprehend with your mind. Your minds are very limited. Use your intuition."
Madeleine L'Engle

The Sensuous Soul

Because the South is about relationships, we cannot go without tapping into the sensuality and intimacy between two people or even the feeling of sensuality with yourself. This isn't about sex, although it can and does include the physical aspect of a relationship. Intimacy is about being vulnerable, heart-centered, and open.

In these modern times, we are so distracted and detached. Most often I see people glued to their devices while sitting at a table with live humans. We have lost the art of conversation, of sharing a moment, and creating intimacy within the moment.

This week, I want you to breathe life back into these two elements. Be brave with yourself and with others. Look for moments to create a connection, a real connection with another. Experience the sensual side of yourself, explore what that means to you and how that can be translated into your relationship, either with yourself or with another.

"To be sensual, I think, is to respect and rejoice in the force of life, of life itself, and to be present in all that one does, from the effort of loving to the breaking of bread."
James Baldwin

Ways I love to be loved

Write down all the ways in which you love to be shown love.

Soul Tip : To get you started, think about your senses and explore how they can be employed in finding ways to love you. Revisit your joy list, is there anything on your list that would fill you with love? Use the South Energy of creativity and imagination to get super creative with this list. Share it with someone close to you if that feels right to you.

1. ....
2. ....
3. ....
4. ....
5. ....
6. ....
7. ....
8. ....
9. ....
10. ....
11. ....
12. ....
13. ....
14. ....
15. ....
16. ....
17. ....
18. ....
19. ....
20. ....
21. ....
22. ....
23. ....
24. ....
25. ....

26. ....
27. ....
28. ....
29. ....
30. ....
31. ....
32. ....
33. ....
34. ....
35. ....
36. ....
37. ....
38. ....
39. ....
40. ....
41. ....
42. ....
43. ....
44. ....
45. ....
46. ....
47. ....
48. ....
49. ....
50. ....

Soul Date Plan:

Self Love:

Self Care:

....

....

....

....

....

Relationship to Self

Connect With:

Nurture:

Set Boundaries:

....

....

....

....

....

Relationship to Others

Start:

Continue On:

Finish:

....

....

....

....

....

Relationship to Goals

WEEKLY OVERVIEW

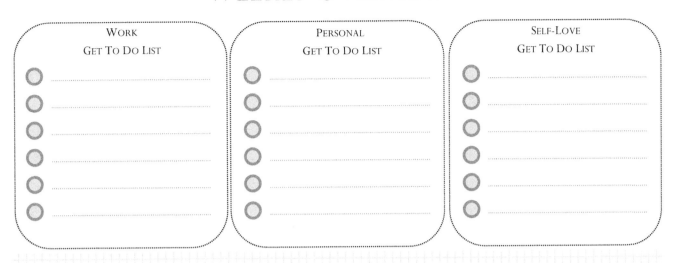

WORK
GET TO DO LIST

PERSONAL
GET TO DO LIST

SELF-LOVE
GET TO DO LIST

EMOTION CHECK IN

What emotion ruled your day?

M
T
W
T
F
S
S

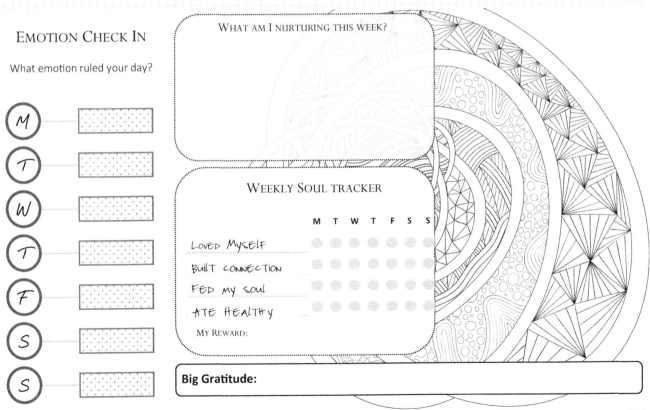

WHAT AM I NURTURING THIS WEEK?

WEEKLY SOUL TRACKER

	M	T	W	T	F	S	S
LOVED MYSELF							
BUILT CONNECTION							
FED MY SOUL							
ATE HEALTHY							

MY REWARD:

Big Gratitude:

Empowering

I am ...

Nurturing

Date:

TODAY

05
06
07
08
09
10
11
12
01
02
03
04
05
06
07
08
09
10
11
12

MORNING MANTRA/PRAYER:

SELF LOVE/CARE

INTUITIVE MESSAGES

TODAY'S GRATITUDE:

DAILY LOVE WARRIOR CHALLENGE:

Carve out a moment to nurture your relationship today. If you are single, then nurture yourself. If you are with a partner, then connect with them and nurture the relationship in a way that allows both of you to connect.

DAILY LOVE REFLECTIVE QUESTION:

My favorite way to spend time with a loved one is …

Empowering

I learned ...

Nurturing

Date:

TODAY

05
06
07
08
09
10
11
12
01
02
03
04
05
06
07
08
09
10
11
12

Morning Mantra/Prayer:

Self Love/Care

Intuitive Messages

Today's Gratitude:

Daily Love Warrior Challenge:

Ask questions. Find out something new about your partner (or someone close to you) by asking various questions to discover a new fact. Be curious and make it about them, not about your story.

Daily Love reflective question:

What do you need/want most from an intimate relationship?

Empowering

I loved well by ...

Nurturing

Date:

TODAY

05
06
07
08
09
10
11
12
01
02
03
04
05
06
07
08
09
10
11
12

MORNING MANTRA/PRAYER:

SELF LOVE/CARE

INTUITIVE MESSAGES

TODAY'S GRATITUDE:

DAILY LOVE WARRIOR CHALLENGE:

Dress confidently today. Find moments throughout the day where you can be both confident and vulnerable, sexy and assertive, creative and grounded. See how it feels to be in command of your day and in every situation. Ask for what you want.

DAILY LOVE REFLECTIVE QUESTION:

When do you feel sexy?

Empowering

I felt ...

Nurturing

Date:

TODAY

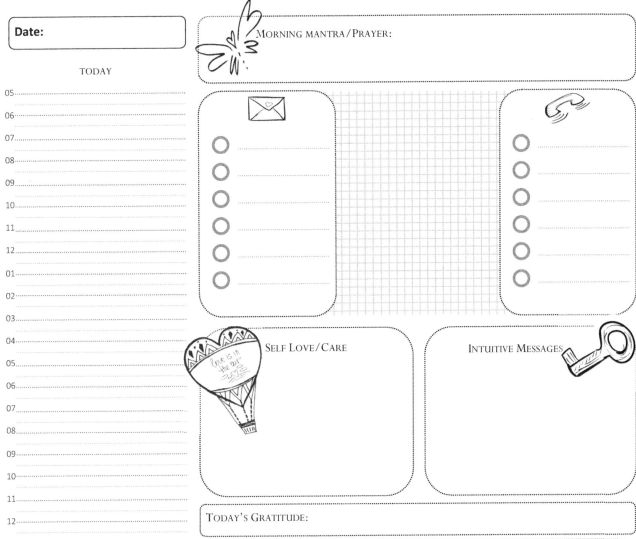

MORNING MANTRA/PRAYER:

05
06
07
08
09
10
11
12
01
02
03
04
05
06
07
08
09
10
11
12

SELF LOVE/CARE

INTUITIVE MESSAGES

TODAY'S GRATITUDE:

DAILY LOVE WARRIOR CHALLENGE:

Pleasure yourself with the pure intention of feeling your own body and not with the intention of going right for the Big O. Take your time, feel your muscles and skin, tease yourself, try something new, linger, change rhythms, make it different and erotic.

DAILY LOVE REFLECTIVE QUESTION:

What turns you on sexually?

Empowering

I felt ...

Nurturing

Date:

TODAY

MORNING MANTRA/PRAYER:

05
06
07
08
09
10
11
12
01
02
03
04
05
06
07
08
09
10
11
12

SELF LOVE/CARE

INTUITIVE MESSAGES

TODAY'S GRATITUDE:

DAILY LOVE WARRIOR CHALLENGE:

Together, with someone important to you in your life, create a ritual that will open sacred space for you both. Once you have created sacred space, invite each other to share honestly about what is in your heart.

DAILY LOVE REFLECTIVE QUESTION:

Do you feel spiritually connected to your partner? Why or why not?

Empowering

I manifested ...

Nurturing

Date:

TODAY

05..
06..
07..
08..
09..
10..
11..
12..
01..
02..
03..
04..
05..
06..
07..
08..
09..
10..
11..
12..

MORNING MANTRA/PRAYER:

○ ....
○ ....
○ ....
○ ....
○ ....
○ ....

○ ....
○ ....
○ ....
○ ....
○ ....
○ ....

SELF LOVE/CARE

INTUITIVE MESSAGES

TODAY'S GRATITUDE:

DAILY LOVE WARRIOR CHALLENGE:

Create a date night plan for you and a loved one. Choose all activities where you will be engaged with each other and not distracted by something else (i.e. no movies!).

DAILY LOVE REFLECTIVE QUESTION:

What is the most difficult part about being vulnerable with another?

Empowering

I was inspired by ...

Nurturing

Date:

TODAY

MORNING MANTRA/PRAYER:

05
06
07
08
09
10
11
12
01
02
03
04
05
06
07
08
09
10
11
12

SELF LOVE/CARE

INTUITIVE MESSAGES

TODAY'S GRATITUDE:

DAILY LOVE WARRIOR CHALLENGE:

Write a love letter to either your partner, a friend or someone important to you, or to yourself. Allow yourself to be heart-centered, open, and vulnerable in what you share.

DAILY LOVE REFLECTIVE QUESTION:

What do you wish you could tell your partner?

Empowering

I created ...

Nurturing

Date:

TODAY

Morning Mantra/Prayer:

05
06
07
08
09
10
11
12
01
02
03
04
05
06
07
08
09
10
11
12

SELF LOVE/CARE

INTUITIVE MESSAGES

TODAY'S GRATITUDE:

DAILY LOVE WARRIOR CHALLENGE:

If you have a partner who you feel comfortable and safe with, ask for a night of intimacy without sex. Spend the time getting to know each other's body, and heart, without the pressure of taking it further. Gaze into each other's eyes, touch, use all of your senses to experience the moment.

DAILY LOVE REFLECTIVE QUESTION:

What are you willing to do or not do in your relationship?

Insights from my

meditation

Suggested Weekly Meditation: *Sacred Love* | www.dakotaearthcloud.com

Date:

Meditation:

Primary Message I Received

I spoke to a tree   and it said to me...

LOOK FOR SIGNS

Throughout the week, be aware of signs, messages, insights that you receive. Log them here.

Aho Mitakuye Oyasin

Weekly Check-In

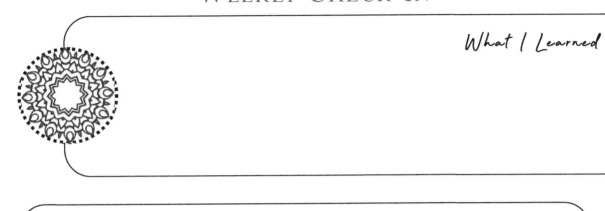

What I Learned

My Big Wins

My Challenges

Sum Up This Week in 4-5 Words

"All have senses, but not all have sensuality because sensuality is predicated on one's soul journey to self awareness."
Lebo Grand

Awakening My Heart

Life is meant to be lived from a heart-opened, heart-centered, heart-awakened space. It is only from this vantage point where we can connect with others from an authentic place that is full of truth, presence, and healing. It happens like a tiny prick at first, we dip our toes into the world of vulnerability and in the beginning, we are full of trepidation. But then we are invited inward, and we learn that in those moments we allowed the opening, we came undone. In that undoing, we find a sense of wholeness.

Living from this place is succulent, rich, and worth the journey.

"For a seed to achieve its greatest expression, it must come completely undone. The shell cracks, its insides come out and everything changes. To someone who doesn't understand growth, it would look like complete destruction."
Cynthia Occelli

Heart-Centered, Heart-Awakened Living

Write down all the ways you can imagine your life looking if you were living
heart-centered and heart-awakened. What if ...

1 ....
2 ....
3 ....
4 ....
5 ....
6 ....
7 ....
8 ....
9 ....
10 ....
11 ....
12 ....
13 ....
14 ....
15 ....
16 ....
17 ....
18 ....
19 ....
20 ....
21 ....
22 ....
23 ....
24 ....
25 ....

26 ....
27 ....
28 ....
29 ....
30 ....
31 ....
32 ....
33 ....
34 ....
35 ....
36 ....
37 ....
38 ....
39 ....
40 ....
41 ....
42 ....
43 ....
44 ....
45 ....
46 ....
47 ....
48 ....
49 ....
50 ....

Soul Date Plan:

....

....

....

....

....

Self Love:

....

....

....

....

....

Self Care:

....

....

....

....

....

Relationship to Self

Connect With:

....

....

....

....

....

Nurture:

....

....

....

....

....

Set Boundaries:

....

....

....

....

....

Relationship to Others

Start:

....

....

....

....

....

Continue On:

....

....

....

....

....

Finish:

....

....

....

....

....

Relationship to Goals

WEEKLY OVERVIEW

WORK
GET TO DO LIST

PERSONAL
GET TO DO LIST

SELF-LOVE
GET TO DO LIST

EMOTION CHECK IN

What emotion ruled your day?

M
T
W
T
F
S
S

WHAT AM I NURTURING THIS WEEK?

WEEKLY SOUL TRACKER

	M	T	W	T	F	S	S
LOVED MYSELF							
BUILT CONNECTION							
FED MY SOUL							
ATE HEALTHY							

MY REWARD:

Big Gratitude:

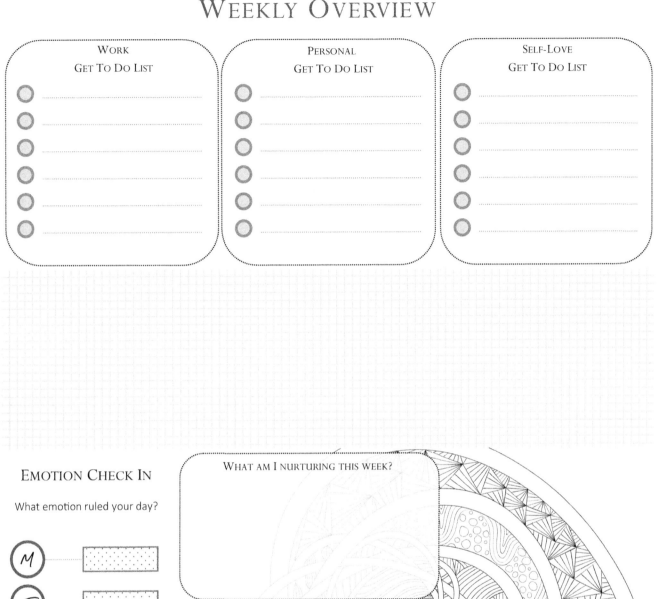

Empowering

I am ...

Nurturing

Date:

TODAY

05
06
07
08
09
10
11
12
01
02
03
04
05
06
07
08
09
10
11
12

MORNING MANTRA/PRAYER:

○
○
○
○
○
○
○

○
○
○
○
○
○

SELF LOVE/CARE

INTUITIVE MESSAGES

TODAY'S GRATITUDE:

DAILY LOVE WARRIOR CHALLENGE:

As you move through your interactions today, notice whether you comply with how others see you or withholding who you are. Find a moment where you can bravely be you.

DAILY LOVE REFLECTIVE QUESTION:

How would it look if you lived life from a heart-centered space?

Empowering

I learned ...

Nurturing

Date:

TODAY

MORNING MANTRA/PRAYER:

05
06
07
08
09
10
11
12
01
02
03
04
05
06
07
08
09
10
11
12

SELF LOVE/CARE

INTUITIVE MESSAGES

TODAY'S GRATITUDE:

DAILY LOVE WARRIOR CHALLENGE:

Choose a trait that makes you feel good about who you are: your laugh, ability to smile, conversation skills. Look for a moment today to interject that part of you and see how others react to

DAILY LOVE REFLECTIVE QUESTION:

How does it feel to be celebrated and accepted for who you truly are?

Empowering

I loved well by ...

Nurturing

Date:

TODAY

05
06
07
08
09
10
11
12
01
02
03
04
05
06
07
08
09
10
11
12

MORNING MANTRA/PRAYER:

SELF LOVE/CARE

INTUITIVE MESSAGES

TODAY'S GRATITUDE:

DAILY LOVE WARRIOR CHALLENGE:

Spend time in nature today and observe the relationship between the elements contained in a space—how the tree interacts with the earth and nearby plants. Imagine you being a part of

DAILY LOVE REFLECTIVE QUESTION:

What shuts your heart down? What opens your heart?

Empowering

I felt ...

Nurturing

Date:

TODAY

MORNING MANTRA/PRAYER:

05
06
07
08
09
10
11
12
01
02
03
04
05
06
07
08
09
10
11
12

SELF LOVE/CARE

INTUITIVE MESSAGES

TODAY'S GRATITUDE:

DAILY LOVE WARRIOR CHALLENGE:

Find a moment to be vulnerable with another today. Let yourself trust openly, speak compassionately and be present. How does this strengthen your relationship to this person?

DAILY LOVE REFLECTIVE QUESTION:

What happens inside you when you deny yourself an open heart or being vulnerable?

Empowering

I manifested ...

Nurturing

Date:

TODAY

05
06
07
08
09
10
11
12
01
02
03
04
05
06
07
08
09
10
11
12

MORNING MANTRA/PRAYER:

SELF LOVE/CARE

INTUITIVE MESSAGES

TODAY'S GRATITUDE:

DAILY LOVE WARRIOR CHALLENGE:

Perform a random act of kindness today. One of the easiest ways to open the heart is to give unconditionally and from love, to another human or animal. Pick your moment (s) to do kind-

DAILY LOVE REFLECTIVE QUESTION:

What prevents you from expressing your needs and desires? What are you afraid of?

Empowering

I was inspired by ...

Nurturing

Date:

TODAY

MORNING MANTRA/PRAYER:

05.....................................
06.....................................
07.....................................
08.....................................
09.....................................
10.....................................
11.....................................
12.....................................
01.....................................
02.....................................
03.....................................
04.....................................
05.....................................
06.....................................
07.....................................
08.....................................
09.....................................
10.....................................
11.....................................
12.....................................

SELF LOVE/CARE

INTUITIVE MESSAGES

TODAY'S GRATITUDE:

DAILY LOVE WARRIOR CHALLENGE:

Make a playlist of heart opening music (Deva Premal, Ashana are a few examples). Light candles, draw a bath or create sacred space, turn on the music, and spend time meditating or jour-

DAILY LOVE REFLECTIVE QUESTION:

What invokes a sense of love for you?

Empowering

I created ...

Nurturing

Date:

TODAY

05
06
07
08
09
10
11
12
01
02
03
04
05
06
07
08
09
10
11
12

MORNING MANTRA/PRAYER:

SELF LOVE/CARE

INTUITIVE MESSAGES

TODAY'S GRATITUDE:

DAILY LOVE WARRIOR CHALLENGE:

Write a love letter to your younger self. What did you need to hear when you were growing up? Nurture that part of yourself that still needs to hear that.

DAILY LOVE REFLECTIVE QUESTION:

Is there anyone you need to forgive so you can make space in your heart for love?

Insights from my

meditation

Suggested Weekly Meditation: *Opening the Heart Center (Apple Tree)* | www.dakotaearthcloud.com

Date:

Meditation:

Primary Message I Received

I spoke to a tree   and it said to me...

LOOK FOR SIGNS

Throughout the week, be aware of signs, messages, insights that you receive. Log them here.

Aho Mitakuye Oyasin

WEEKLY CHECK-IN

What I Learned

My Big Wins

My Challenges

Sum Up This Week in 4-5 Words

"Awakening in Love is realizing Love is You, Love is Everyone, Love is All."
— *Wald Wassermann*

Soul Tracking

In each of the directions, there are certain tools which can be used for interpreting and receiving messages from our Spirit Guides. In the South Direction, we use our heightened intuition which has a tie into the North Direction, we also strengthen our self-love muscle so we learn to trust our intuition more. We add play into our schedule, messages are much harder to receive if you are stressed and overwhelmed. And nature, nature is a tremendous conduit for receiving messages.

The more time you spend in nature, the more connected you will become to your soul's language and the reception for messages will be enhanced.

"You are free, you are powerful, you are good, you are love, you have value, you have a purpose. All is well."

11

Beautiful Things

Write down all the beautiful things you have witnessed so far in this lifetime.

1 ....
2 ....
3 ....
4 ....
5 ....
6 ....
7 ....
8 ....
9 ....
10 ....
11 ....
12 ....
13 ....
14 ....
15 ....
16 ....
17 ....
18 ....
19 ....
20 ....
21 ....
22 ....
23 ....
24 ....
25 ....

26 ....
27 ....
28 ....
29 ....
30 ....
31 ....
32 ....
33 ....
34 ....
35 ....
36 ....
37 ....
38 ....
39 ....
40 ....
41 ....
42 ....
43 ....
44 ....
45 ....
46 ....
47 ....
48 ....
49 ....
50 ....

Soul Date Plan: **Self Love:**   **Self Care:**

....

....

....

....

....

Relationship to Self

Connect With: **Nurture:**   **Set Boundaries:**

....

....

....

....

....

Relationship to Others

Start: **Continue On:**   **Finish:**

....

....

....

....

....

Relationship to Goals

WEEKLY OVERVIEW

WORK
GET TO DO LIST

- ○
- ○
- ○
- ○
- ○
- ○

PERSONAL
GET TO DO LIST

- ○
- ○
- ○
- ○
- ○
- ○

SELF-LOVE
GET TO DO LIST

- ○
- ○
- ○
- ○
- ○
- ○

EMOTION CHECK IN

What emotion ruled your day?

- M
- T
- W
- T
- F
- S
- S

WHAT AM I NURTURING THIS WEEK?

WEEKLY SOUL TRACKER

	M	T	W	T	F	S	S
LOVED MYSELF							
BUILT CONNECTION							
FED MY SOUL							
ATE HEALTHY							

MY REWARD:

Big Gratitude:

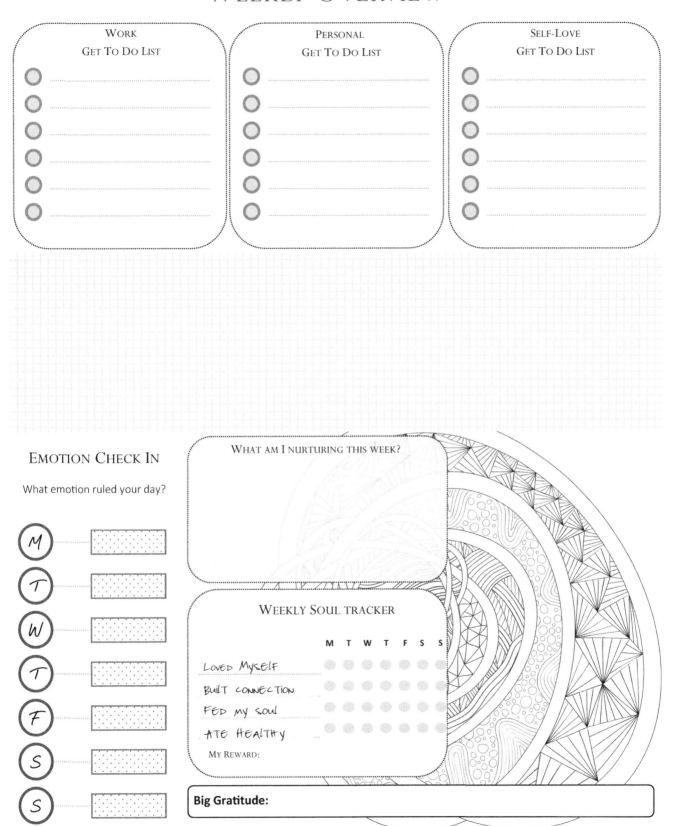

Empowering

I am ...

Nurturing

Date:

TODAY

MORNING MANTRA/PRAYER:

05
06
07
08
09
10
11
12
01
02
03
04
05
06
07
08
09
10
11
12

SELF LOVE/CARE

INTUITIVE MESSAGES

TODAY'S GRATITUDE:

DAILY LOVE WARRIOR CHALLENGE:

Focus on words today. Take a journal with you and jot down any words (spoken or read) that capture your attention. Once the day is finished, look at your list—do you see a pattern? Can you form a message from them?

DAILY LOVE REFLECTIVE QUESTION:

How have you grown?

Empowering

I learned ...

Nurturing

Date:

TODAY

MORNING MANTRA/PRAYER:

05

06

07

08

09

10

11

12

01

02

03

04

05

06

07

08

09

10

11

12

SELF LOVE/CARE

INTUITIVE MESSAGES

TODAY'S GRATITUDE:

DAILY LOVE WARRIOR CHALLENGE:

Pay attention to the shift in your energy whenever you enter a new space, or are around various people. How does your energy fluctuate? Do you feel it shift in different chakras?

DAILY LOVE REFLECTIVE QUESTION:

What emotion would you like to experience more in your life? How would that change you?

Empowering

I loved well by ...

Nurturing

Date:

TODAY

MORNING MANTRA/PRAYER:

05
06
07
08
09
10
11
12
01
02
03
04
05
06
07
08
09
10
11
12

SELF LOVE/CARE

INTUITIVE MESSAGES

TODAY'S GRATITUDE:

DAILY LOVE WARRIOR CHALLENGE:

Sit with a tree today and connect to it, see if you can (hear, feel, intuit, see) any messages the tree has for you.

DAILY LOVE REFLECTIVE QUESTION:

What have you learned about yourself?

Empowering

Nurturing

Date:

TODAY

MORNING MANTRA/PRAYER:

05
06
07
08
09
10
11
12
01
02
03
04
05
06
07
08
09
10
11
12

SELF LOVE/CARE

INTUITIVE MESSAGES

TODAY'S GRATITUDE:

DAILY LOVE WARRIOR CHALLENGE:

Grab your colored markers/pencils and your journal. Doodle all the symbols and shapes you remember seeing today. Once you finish, look for any patterns or overall messages.

DAILY LOVE REFLECTIVE QUESTION:

What blocks/fears do you still need to work through?

Empowering

I manifested ...

Nurturing

Date:

TODAY

MORNING MANTRA/PRAYER:

05
06
07
08
09
10
11
12
01
02
03
04
05
06
07
08
09
10
11
12

SELF LOVE/CARE

INTUITIVE MESSAGES

TODAY'S GRATITUDE:

DAILY LOVE WARRIOR CHALLENGE:

Eaves drop on different conversations today and pick up various lines, write them down. At he end of the day, compile them together to look for any themes, patterns, or messages.

DAILY LOVE REFLECTIVE QUESTION:

What tools or energies of the South do you want to implement more into your life?

Empowering

I was inspired by ...

Nurturing

Date:

TODAY

05
06
07
08
09
10
11
12
01
02
03
04
05
06
07
08
09
10
11
12

MORNING MANTRA/PRAYER:

SELF LOVE/CARE

INTUITIVE MESSAGES

TODAY'S GRATITUDE:

DAILY LOVE WARRIOR CHALLENGE:

Take a trip to the bookstore or library. Look for titles that "speak" to you and open to a random page, what word or sentence "pops" out to you? Gather a handful of these and look for messages, themes, or patterns. Do they answer a question you have had?

DAILY LOVE REFLECTIVE QUESTION:

What has been the loudest message for you during this direction?

 Empowering

I created ...

Nurturing

Date:

TODAY

05
06
07
08
09
10
11
12
01
02
03
04
05
06
07
08
09
10
11
12

MORNING MANTRA/PRAYER:

SELF LOVE/CARE

INTUITIVE MESSAGES

TODAY'S GRATITUDE:

DAILY LOVE WARRIOR CHALLENGE:

Pay attention to any animals that come across your path today. What medicine or message do they bring to you? Did you see one more than 3 times?

DAILY LOVE REFLECTIVE QUESTION:

Where do you need more ease/flow in your life?

Insights from my meditation

Suggested Weekly Meditation: *Seven Sacred Pools* | www.dakotaearthcloud.com

Date:

Meditation:

Primary Message I Received

LOOK FOR SIGNS

Throughout the week, be aware of signs, messages, insights that you receive. Log them here.

Aho Mitakuye Oyasin

WEEKLY CHECK-IN

What I Learned

My Big Wins

My Challenges

Sum Up This Week in 4-5 Words

"Awakening in Love is realizing Love is You, Love is Everyone, Love is All."
— Wald Wassermann

Dancing into Harvest

In this final week of the South Direction, we begin turning our focus towards the West Direction and begin building the bridge between these two directions. Bringing our relationships into the west to create healthy boundaries, extending self-love in the way that we care for body and health, opening our heart space to fully feel gratitude, and seeing the seeds we nurtured manifest into a bounty of abundance in our world.

"Surround yourself with people who empower you to become better." Anonymous

A Vibrant Life

Write down all the ways your life is vibrant, rich, creative, and awesome!

1 ....
2 ....
3 ....
4 ....
5 ....
6 ....
7 ....
8 ....
9 ....
10 ....
11 ....
12 ....
13 ....
14 ....
15 ....
16 ....
17 ....
18 ....
19 ....
20 ....
21 ....
22 ....
23 ....
24 ....
25 ....

26 ....
27 ....
28 ....
29 ....
30 ....
31 ....
32 ....
33 ....
34 ....
35 ....
36 ....
37 ....
38 ....
39 ....
40 ....
41 ....
42 ....
43 ....
44 ....
45 ....
46 ....
47 ....
48 ....
49 ....
50 ....

Soul Date Plan:

Self Love:

Self Care:

....
....
....
....
....

Relationship to Self

Connect With:

Nurture:

Set Boundaries:

....
....
....
....
....

Relationship to Others

Start:

Continue On:

Finish:

....
....
....
....
....

Relationship to Goals

WEEKLY OVERVIEW

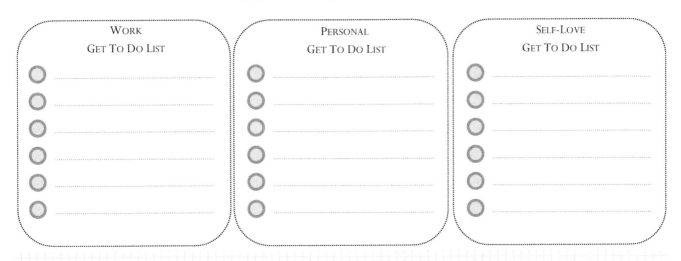

WORK
GET TO DO LIST

○ ....
○ ....
○ ....
○ ....
○ ....
○ ....

PERSONAL
GET TO DO LIST

○ ....
○ ....
○ ....
○ ....
○ ....
○ ....

SELF-LOVE
GET TO DO LIST

○ ....
○ ....
○ ....
○ ....
○ ....
○ ....

EMOTION CHECK IN

What emotion ruled your day?

M
T
W
T
F
S
S

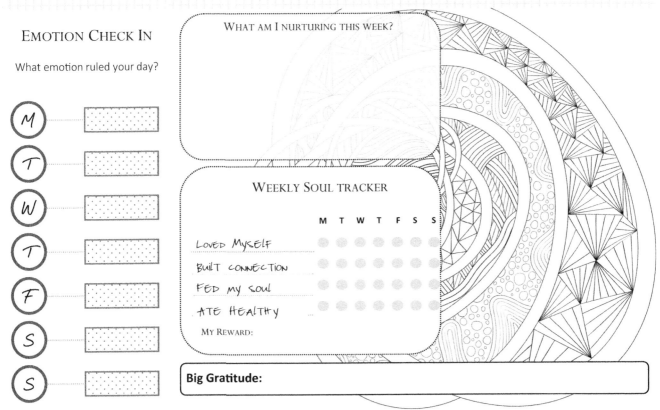

WHAT AM I NURTURING THIS WEEK?

WEEKLY SOUL TRACKER

	M	T	W	T	F	S	S
LOVED MYSELF							
BUILT CONNECTION							
FED MY SOUL							
ATE HEALTHY							

MY REWARD:

Big Gratitude:

Empowering

I am ...

Nurturing

Date:

TODAY

05
06
07
08
09
10
11
12
01
02
03
04
05
06
07
08
09
10
11
12

MORNING MANTRA/PRAYER:

SELF LOVE/CARE

INTUITIVE MESSAGES

TODAY'S GRATITUDE:

DAILY LOVE WARRIOR CHALLENGE:

Revisit your goals, do an assessment—how are you doing? What are the next micro steps you need to be taking?

DAILY LOVE REFLECTIVE QUESTION:

Which relationships sustain you most and are most grateful for? Why?

Empowering

I learned ...

Nurturing

Date:

TODAY

05
06
07
08
09
10
11
12
01
02
03
04
05
06
07
08
09
10
11
12

MORNING MANTRA/PRAYER:

○
○
○
○
○
○

○
○
○
○
○
○

SELF LOVE/CARE

INTUITIVE MESSAGES

TODAY'S GRATITUDE:

DAILY LOVE WARRIOR CHALLENGE:

Prepare your altar for the West Direction. Clean the items from the South Direction, give gratitude for the space they held, the meaning they hold for you. Dust and physically clean the space, smudge, and let it "air" out until you are ready for the Alchemist Direction.

DAILY LOVE REFLECTIVE QUESTION:

Which relationships lack boundaries for you?

Empowering

I loved well by ...

Nurturing

Date:

TODAY

05
06
07
08
09
10
11
12
01
02
03
04
05
06
07
08
09
10
11
12

MORNING MANTRA/PRAYER:

SELF LOVE/CARE

INTUITIVE MESSAGES

TODAY'S GRATITUDE:

DAILY LOVE WARRIOR CHALLENGE:

Order your next workbook for the Alchemist Direction to continue this journey around the Medicine Wheel. All Directional workbooks can be found on your Amazon by searching for Dakota Earth Cloud Walker—and tell your friends!

DAILY LOVE REFLECTIVE QUESTION:

What is most abundant in your South Direction energy?

Empowering

I felt ...

Nurturing

Date:

TODAY

MORNING MANTRA/PRAYER:

05

06

07

08

09

10

11

12

01

02

03

04

05

06

07

08

09

10

11

12

SELF LOVE/CARE

INTUITIVE MESSAGES

TODAY'S GRATITUDE:

DAILY LOVE WARRIOR CHALLENGE:

Tell at least four people why you are grateful for them. Speak from your heart, and speak it in person—either on the phone or in person, not in a text message or email!

DAILY LOVE REFLECTIVE QUESTION:

How is nature speaking to you today?

Empowering

I manifested ...

Nurturing

Date:

TODAY

05
06
07
08
09
10
11
12
01
02
03
04
05
06
07
08
09
10
11
12

MORNING MANTRA/PRAYER:

○
○
○
○
○
○

○
○
○
○
○
○

SELF LOVE/CARE

INTUITIVE MESSAGES

TODAY'S GRATITUDE:

DAILY LOVE WARRIOR CHALLENGE:

Create some form of art today—you might cook a healthy meal, take paints to a canvas, color in this book, create a new space ... whatever speaks to you. Create it with love.

DAILY LOVE REFLECTIVE QUESTION:

What are you creating?

Empowering

I was inspired by ...

Nurturing

Date:

TODAY

05
06
07
08
09
10
11
12
01
02
03
04
05
06
07
08
09
10
11
12

MORNING MANTRA/PRAYER:

SELF LOVE/CARE

INTUITIVE MESSAGES

TODAY'S GRATITUDE:

DAILY LOVE WARRIOR CHALLENGE:

Visit a Farmer's Market and buy fresh, colorful food and cook a healthy, nutritious dinner with your findings. Invite over some friends to participate in your feast with you.

DAILY LOVE REFLECTIVE QUESTION:

What do you want to take from the South into the West Direction and continue working on?

Empowering

I created ...

Nurturing

Date:

TODAY

05
06
07
08
09
10
11
12
01
02
03
04
05
06
07
08
09
10
11
12

MORNING MANTRA/PRAYER:

○
○
○
○
○
○

○
○
○
○
○
○

SELF LOVE/CARE

INTUITIVE MESSAGES

TODAY'S GRATITUDE:

DAILY LOVE WARRIOR CHALLENGE:

Create a closing ceremony/ritual to close out the South Direction for yourself. Give gratitude, be present, and utilize whatever elements feel natural to you.

DAILY LOVE REFLECTIVE QUESTION:

What is the one thing, right now, that you are totally sure of?

Insights from my

meditation

Suggested Weekly Meditation: *Empowering the Soul* | www.dakotaearthcloud.com

Date:

Meditation:

Primary Message I Received

I spoke to a tree and it said to me ...

LOOK FOR SIGNS

Throughout the week, be aware of signs, messages, insights that you receive. Log them here.

Aho Mitakuye Oyasin

WEEKLY CHECK-IN

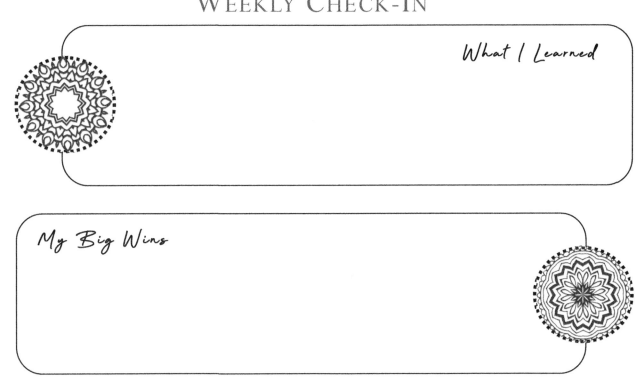

What I Learned

My Big Wins

My Challenges

Sum Up This Week in 4-5 Words

"Awakening in Love is realizing Love is You, Love is Everyone, Love is All."
— Wald Wassermann

Journal and Notes

Use this section of the journal to take notes, journal your thoughts, doodle, add more "get to" lists and whatever else you would like to add!

Notes Date:

Notes Date:

Notes Date:

Notes Date:

Notes Date:

Notes Date:

Notes Date:

Notes Date:

Notes Date:

Notes Date:

Notes Date:

Notes Date:

Notes Date:

Notes Date:

Notes Date:

Notes Date:

Notes Date:

Notes Date:

Notes Date:

Notes Date:

Notes Date:

Notes Date:

Notes Date:

Notes Date:

Made in the USA
Monee, IL
28 June 2022

98745318R00236